DISCOVER CANADA

Saskatchewan

By Dave Margoshes

Consultants

Desmond Morton, FRSC, Professor of History, University of Toronto

J. William Brennan, Ph.D., Department of History, University of Regina

Rosella Mitchell, Consultant, Saskatchewan Education, Regina

Grolier Limited
TORONTO

Winter scene near Mayfair in west central Saskatchewan
Overleaf: **Prairie sunset**

Canadian Cataloguing in Publication Data

Margoshes, Dave, 1941-
  Saskatchewan

(Discover Canada)
Rev. ed.
Includes index.
ISBN 0-7172-3135-6

1. Saskatchewan — Juvenile literature. I. Title.
II. Series : Discover Canada (Toronto, Ont.)

FC3511.2.M3 1996   j971.24   C96-931029-3
F1071.4.M3 1996

Printed and bound in Canada.
Published simultaneously in the United States.
2 3 4 5 6 7 8 9 10 DWF 99 98 97 96

Front cover: Looking across the South Saskatchewan River at Saskatoon
Back cover: Autumn in the Thickwood Hills

Scarth St. Mall, Regina

Table of Contents

Chapter 1   Saskatchewan — The Wheat Province......7
Chapter 2   The Land......9
Chapter 3   The People......17
Chapter 4   The First Inhabitants......23
Chapter 5   The Northwest Rebellion......33
Chapter 6   The Last Best West......45
Chapter 7   The CCF Years to the Present......59
Chapter 8   Government......67
Chapter 9   The Economy......73
Chapter 10   Arts and Recreation......83
Chapter 11   Around the Province......93
Facts at a Glance......105
Maps.......122
Index......125

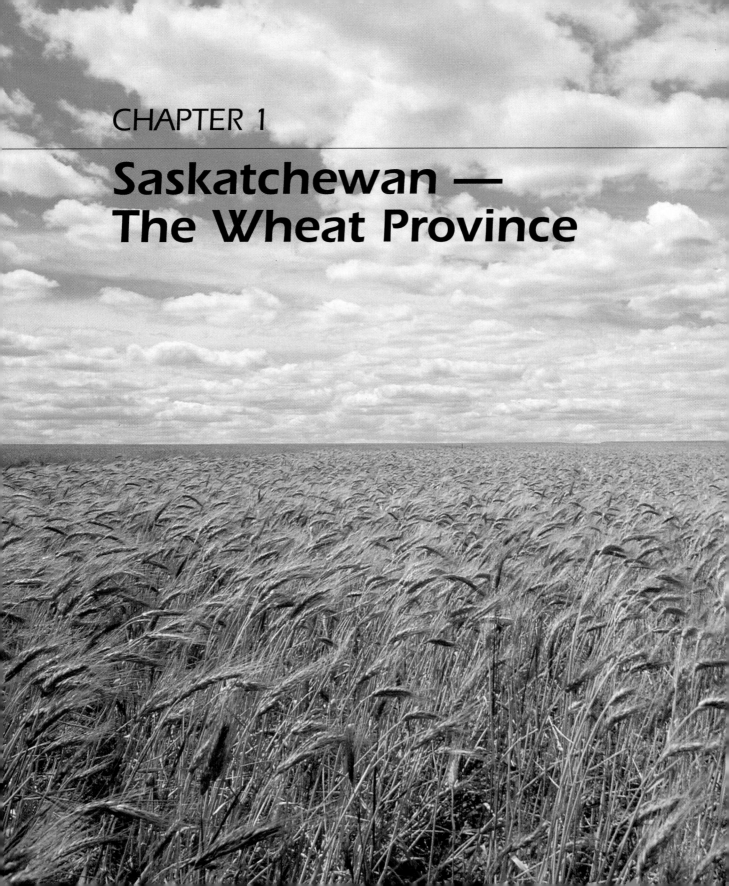

CHAPTER 1

Saskatchewan —
The Wheat Province

Saskatchewan is commonly known as the Wheat Province. Over the years, it has also been called the Breadbasket of Canada, the Breadbasket of the British Empire — even the Breadbasket of the World. All these nicknames reflect the vital role of wheat in Saskatchewan's economy and in the public imagination. Indeed, the image of the province that most quickly springs to mind is of golden wheat fields, shimmering in the sun beneath a vast, cloudless sky.

But Saskatchewan is much more than wheat and farmers. It's also cowboys and coal miners, oil riggers and computer programmers; goose flyways, badlands, sand dunes and cities; Native Indians, Métis and immigrants from dozens of countries around the world; great rivers and dense forests, unforgettable sunsets and mesmerizing northern lights.

In fact, there are two Saskatchewans: the southern half, where 95 percent of the population lives, and the north, a land of rock, evergreen forests and pure, crystal lakes that remains much as it has been for centuries — a land that many Saskatchewanians have never even seen.

The southern plains, of course, have been drastically altered by agriculture and settlement, and little of the original shortgrass prairie remains. Still, it's possible to gaze across a rippling field of wheat and imagine the way it once was, the way W.O. Mitchell described it in his novel *Who Has Seen the Wind:* "Here was the least common denominator of nature, the skeleton requirements simply, of land and sky — Saskatchewan prairie."

Wheat country

CHAPTER 2
The Land

Early European visitors to the area now called Saskatchewan described it as a vast and empty land. Vast it certainly was, but far from empty. Thousands of aboriginal people lived on the flat and gently rolling grasslands of the south, in the wooded central portions and in the rugged, lake-dotted northern forests. The rich soils of the southern and central regions have proven to be some of the most fertile farmland in the country. And beneath the land are large deposits of valuable minerals and metals.

The central of the three Prairie Provinces, Saskatchewan lies just north and west of the centre of the North American continent. Its area of 652 330 square kilometres (251 885 square miles) makes it the fifth-largest of the provinces. Of that area, about 15 percent is water, and more than a third of the rest is forest.

Taking Shape

Because Saskatchewan's history as a province of Canada goes back only to 1905, it's easy to forget that the land itself is hundreds of millions of years old.

During the long prehistory of Saskatchewan, five major geological events occurred that have formed the place we now know. The first dates back almost two billion years to a time when the cooling planet was still finding its shape. It involved the collision of moving plates of the Earth's surface, creating chains of volcanic islands and eventually a range of mountains. About 300

Much of Saskatchewan's park belt, once covered by forests of aspen, poplar and birch, has been cleared for farming.

million years later, shallow seas developed and came to cover most of what is now North America, including Saskatchewan. Over more eons of time, hundreds of primitive life forms developed and multiplied within the warm, salty waters.

The seas gradually receded and land emerged. Thick jungle-like forests grew, and the large land animals known as dinosaurs appeared, about 250 million years ago, to rule Saskatchewan. This was followed, over a period of millions of years, by the decay and breakup of the forests and the spread of grasslands, the extinction of the dinosaurs, and the dominance of mammals. Finally, there was a two-million-year-long period during which almost all of Saskatchewan was at times covered by glaciers; then, the last gradual melting away of the ice.

As recently as 17 000 years ago, the southern edge of the retreating glacier was just north of where Regina now stands. Even 10 000 years ago, when the first archaeological evidence of human presence in Saskatchewan appears, the ice sheet still covered more than a third of the province, not to be completely gone until about 6000 B.C.

These powerful geological forces and events nurtured the development of thousands of different life forms, many of them disappearing as new, more adaptable forms developed. They also

Skeleton of brontothere *Megacerops* at the Royal Saskatchewan Museum. Brontotheres were mammals that lived in the Saskatchewan area over 40 million years ago.

gave Saskatchewan its wealth of mineral resources: coal, oil, natural gas, potash, uranium, silver and gold.

Topography

The province has two major topographical zones, with a transition zone between them.

The southern third of the province is made up almost entirely of dry prairie grasslands, part of the fertile Great Plains that stretch across the heart of the continent all the way south to Texas. While generally flat or rolling and treeless, the Saskatchewan prairie is pockmarked by many tree-fringed sloughs, salt-encrusted potholes and low, sandy hills, and cut by coulees and several river valleys. At the southern edge of this zone, the prairie gives way to a fascinating

Southern Saskatchewan's varied landscapes. *Left:* The Big Muddy Badlands. *Right:* The Great Sand Hills. *Inset:* Prairie fields near Regina

series of topographical features that include sand dunes, rattler-infested badlands and the highest point in Canada between the Rockies and Labrador. Most of the prairie region has been cultivated, with the remainder used as range for cattle.

North of the prairie is a wide transition belt of parkland: rolling hills and valleys, lakes and aspen trees growing in rich black soil left by the last glacier. Large portions of this parkland area have been cleared for agricultural production.

The northern third of the province is part of the Canadian, or Precambrian, Shield, an arc of ancient rock that covers most of central Canada. The soil here is thin and the landscape is dominated by boreal forest of small spruce, tamarack, aspen and birch, and is dotted with innumerable lakes. At the northeastern edge of the province, the trees become smaller and sparser as the land grades to the open tundra of the Arctic region.

Water

Many of Saskatchewan's problems as an agricultural area stem from its chronic lack of moisture, and yet there is plenty of water in

Dunbar Falls in Saskatchewan's Shield country

the province — over 100 000 lakes, rivers and streams, most of them teeming with northern pike, walleye and trout.

Saskatchewan and Alberta are the only provinces that lie within more than two drainage systems. Most of Saskatchewan drains into Hudson Bay through the Churchill River and through the Saskatchewan River system and Lake Winnipeg; the northwest area drains into the Arctic through Lake Athabasca and the Mackenzie River system; in the southwest, a small area drains into the Missouri River and eventually into the Gulf of Mexico.

Most of the province's thousands of lakes are in the north. Lake Athabasca and Reindeer Lake are the fourth and fifth largest lakes totally within Canada. Both lie mainly in Saskatchewan, but a portion of Athabasca is in Alberta, and Reindeer spills into Manitoba. Other large lakes include Wollaston Lake, Cree Lake, Lac La Ronge and, in the south, Lake Diefenbaker, which was created as a reservoir for irrigation purposes.

There are dozens of rivers, but the Churchill and the two branches of the Saskatchewan are the major systems.

Display of fall colours near Battleford. *Inset:* **Winter at Waskesiu Lake, Prince Albert National Park**

Climate

Saskatchewan suffers from long, bitterly cold winters and short, sweltering summers. The lowest temperature on record is -56.7°C (-70°F) and the record high is 45°C (113°F), a national record. Neither winter nor summer seems to be as bad in recent years as oldtimers remember, however — and maybe they're right, since the above temperatures were recorded over fifty years ago. Spring and fall are pleasant, but wind is a constant in all seasons.

The climate is known as continental, with low rain and snowfall, averaging 275 to 500 millimetres (11 to 20 inches) on the plains, and a lot of sunshine. The area is often subject to drought. On the average there are about a hundred frost-free days a year in central Saskatchewan, and no more than 110 in the south.

Mean temperatures recorded in Saskatoon are -19.3°C (-3°F) in January and 18.5°C (65°F) in July. In the far north, winters are considerably colder, and temperatures in the -40s are common.

Wildlife

As the dinosaurs dwindled into extinction some sixty-five million years ago, mammals began to grow, some of them to remarkable size. Fossilized evidence has been discovered of rhinoceros-like animals, sabre-toothed tigers, camels and other animals now extinct — even crocodiles, a good fossil of which, found at Carrot River in 1991, is seven metres (23 feet) long. Mastodons and mammoths, cousins of the elephant, were hunted by early man until around 10 000 years ago. Horses of various sizes lived in the area but disappeared from North America around 6000 B.C., not to return until Europeans reintroduced them in the sixteenth century.

The southern prairies were a perfect habitat for buffalo (more correctly but less commonly called bison), and they in turn influenced the landscape. There were once an estimated 50 to 60 million of them in North America and their migrations in the tens

Far left: **Black-tailed prairie dog. Southwestern Saskatchewan is now the only place in Canada where these sociable little animals build their complex underground "towns."** *Left:* **The pronghorn is the fastest-running animal in North America.** *Inset:* **White pelican**

of thousands ensured that trees had little chance of taking hold. As they became more numerous, the grasslands spread; more grass allowed their numbers to increase. Almost all of them are gone now, the victims of wanton overhunting.

In the north, caribou still move in vast herds, and the boreal forests provide a home to moose, elk, black bears, white-tailed deer and wolves, and to small fur-bearing animals such as beaver, marten and muskrat. In the south, pronghorn antelope bound across the prairie and coyotes can still be heard howling at night in rural areas. The prairie dog, found nowhere else in Canada, can be seen playing in the sun in the southwest, near Val Marie, and the swift fox, once extinct in the province, has been re-established.

The ferruginous hawk and the burrowing owl, which had all but disappeared, have also made remarkable comebacks in recent years, and efforts are being made to reintroduce the peregrine falcon, which had died out entirely. Almost 350 species of birds breed in Saskatchewan, from upland game birds such as partridge, pheasant and the sharp-tailed grouse, or prairie chicken, to waterfowl like the Canada goose, swans, loons, the white pelican and ducks galore — an estimated 25 percent of all ducks in North America are born in Saskatchewan.

CHAPTER 3
The People

Saskatchewan's population stood at 1 020 138 in 1996, divided almost equally between men and women. With 3.65 percent of the Canadian population, Saskatchewan ranks sixth among the provinces. The population density is 1.73 people per square kilometre (2.8 per square mile) — second lowest in the nation.

Almost everyone is connected in some way, even if only through relatives, to agriculture. And yet only 37 percent of the population lives in the country, with about 170 000 people actually on farms. Almost 60 percent of urban dwellers live in either Regina, with 199 000 people, or Saskatoon with 221 000.

First Comers

Henry Kelsey was the first European to set eyes on the wilderness region that would become Saskatchewan. But when he arrived in the area, just over 300 years ago, he was greeted by Native people whose forebears had been living there for 10 000 years or more.

No one knows for sure how many Native people there were in the Saskatchewan area at the time — probably a few thousand, divided into as many as seven nations, which in turn were broken into dozens of smaller bands. They remained undisturbed for at least 150 years after Kelsey's visit, with only a handful of European fur traders, missionaries and explorers wandering into what is now called the Saskatchewan Valley.

It wasn't really until Confederation in 1867 that outsiders began to take Saskatchewan seriously as a place to settle. The first people to establish farms in the area were Métis — people of mixed European and Indian ancestry who had fled the political turmoil that accompanied the birth of Manitoba as a province. They were followed by surveyors who began to divide up a land inhabited largely by people who had never thought of land as something that a person could own.

The young federal government in Ottawa was anxious to fill up the western interior, but for several years could attract only a trickle of settlers. An offer of free land helped, and so did the creation of the North-West Mounted Police, who brought law and order to the West in the mid-1870s. When the railway arrived in 1882 the floodgates to large-scale immigration were wide open.

New Arrivals

An 1881 census showed 19 000 people in the area that now is Saskatchewan. A thousand or so were settlers from Europe or eastern Canada, primarily of British origin; the rest were Indians and Métis. By 1901, the population had grown fourfold to 91 279.

Saskatchewan continued to experience phenomenal growth in its early years as a province. The population exploded to almost half a million by 1911 and to three quarters of a million a decade later. This made Saskatchewan the third most populous province in the country, a distinction it would maintain until the fifties. Free land was the big attraction. People flooded in from areas where good land was scarce — from Russia and the Ukraine, Norway and Sweden, Germany and Finland as well as England and the United States. By 1931, just as the Great Depression was taking hold, the population peaked at 921 785 before beginning a decline that lasted through the war years.

Fuelled by improved economic conditions, however, the population began to recover in the mid-fifties. It crossed the million mark in the mid-eighties before tough times started it on another decline. Immigration declined as well — in 1991, a mere 2430 people came from other countries to make their home in Saskatchewan. Patterns of immigration have changed too. Today, most immigrants come from Asia, Africa, the East and West Indies and Latin America.

Far left: Newly arrived settlers from Eastern Europe. *Left:* Hilda Swedenburg, daughter of Swedish American immigrants

Saskatchewan Today

Saskatchewan is the only province in which people with at least one parent of English or French background make up less than half the population. In the 1991 census, about 23 percent declared themselves to be strictly British in origin, with around 12 percent German, 6 percent Ukrainian, 7 percent Aboriginal peoples and 3 percent French.

Saskatchewan's status Indian population was estimated at 63 000 in 1991, with about half — members of 70 bands — living on the province's 156 reserves. But the total Aboriginal population, including non-status Indians and Métis, was 97 000, or about 10 percent of the total population. This is the fastest growing group in the province.

Given the broad ethnic diversity, it is not surprising that multicultural celebrations are popular in Saskatchewan. Regina's Mosaic and Saskatoon's Folk Fest draw thousands of people attracted by the opportunity to sample the food, crafts, music and dance of many different lands. Several smaller centres, including Melville, Yorkton and Lloydminster, also hold multicultural festivals, and individual cultural groups celebrate their heritage

Multicultural
Saskatchewan on
display during
Regina's three-day
Mosaic festival

throughout the province. There are Ukrainian festivals in Saskatoon, Canora and Prince Albert; a celebration of Icelandic culture in Wynyard, of Scandinavian culture in Weldon; Highland Dancing Championships at North Battleford and a Fête Fransaskoise at Zenon Park. Humboldt honours its German roots with not one but three yearly festivals, and there are powwows at many Indian reserves and in Regina and other urban centres as well.

Despite the ethnic mix, people of Saskatchewan are overwhelmingly English speakers. In 1991, about 85 percent of Saskatchewan residents declared their mother tongue to be English. Among other languages, German led with 4 percent, followed by Ukrainian, French and Cree.

Saskatchewan people are also overwhelmingly Christian, with well over half declaring themselves Protestant, a fourth Roman Catholic and small but significant numbers of adherents to the Ukrainian Catholic and Greek Orthodox faiths. About 2 percent are

The changing times: Langham's old railway station reborn as the town's Senior Citizens' Centre. *Inset:* Seniors get a chance to strut their stuff at the Yorkton Western Development Museum's Threshermen's Show and Seniors' Festival.

Jewish, and there are small numbers belonging to other religions or who have no religious preference. Among the Protestants, the United church is the largest, with over 30 percent of all church members; Anglicans and Lutherans are second and third with about 10 percent each, followed by Mennonites, Presbyterians and Baptists.

Saskatchewan appears to be a healthy place to live. Women there have the highest life expectancy of any Canadians — 80.5 years; men trail behind at 73.7 years, second highest in the country. As a result, the population is aging. The province has the highest proportion of people over 65 in the country.

CHAPTER 4

The First Inhabitants

It is estimated that 15 000 to 50 000 people were living in the northwestern interior of North America 300 years ago. In western Canada, there were three major groups, each with its own language and culture. In the north lived the Athapaskan-speaking Chipewyan, Beaver and Slavey people, also known as the Dene, relying on caribou for food, clothing and tools. South of them were Algonkian speakers, the numerous Cree and Blackfoot of the parkland and central plains, who hunted big game as well as buffalo. And in the extreme south lived the migratory Assiniboine and the Gros Ventre, who spoke Siouan languages and relied almost completely on buffalo.

All of these people had a special relationship with the land. They lived off it in every sense of the word: they hunted, fished, picked fruit and berries, made tools and weapons from bone, wood and stone. They travelled freely across the plains and through the forests in pursuit of the vast herds of buffalo and caribou that were the mainstays of their economies.

The Native Way of Life

The early inhabitants of Saskatchewan left many clues about their lives. They left stories embodying their beliefs and traditions, which have been passed on orally, from generation to generation, down through the centuries to the present. They also left a small but significant number of artworks, dating back hundreds of years.

Skin lodge of an Assiniboine chief

Right: A young boy studies the figures painted hundreds of years ago by his ancestors. *Below:* Tipi ring in Grasslands National Park

Petroglyphs (carvings in rock) in southern Saskatchewan depict faces, animals and animal tracks; pictographs (rock paintings) found along rivers in the north show hunting scenes. Elsewhere, figures of animals and people made of small stones, and medicine wheels, believed to have religious significance, have been found on the prairie. Finally, archaeologists have uncovered the remains of living areas throughout the province. The oldest settlements — the Niska site near Ponteix, and the Heron Eden site near Prelate, both on the southwestern prairie — date back 9000 years. Tipi rings, circles of stones used to hold down the hide covering of tipis, show where dwellings stood. Fire-cracked rocks and pieces of broken pottery reveal cooking areas. Buried animal bones bear mute testimony to killing and butchering spots.

Because of all this, we know that the men hunted, sometimes individually and sometimes in large groups. They went after both large and small animals — including in earliest times elephant-like mastodons and giant woolly mammoths, which they attacked in bogs and at water holes, using spears with stone points. After these animals became extinct, they hunted giant bison, which grew in number as their size gradually diminished. The women gathered a wide variety of naturally growing fruits and vegetables.

They had fire and fashioned their own cooking pots and other utensils, tools and weapons with a high degree of craftsmanship. They lived in small family bands and sometimes larger groupings, and liked music and games and personal ornaments, much as people do today. Their small, easily movable dwellings were made of branches and animal hides, and they used sleds, often pulled by dogs, to transport them. Northerners had canoes and snowshoes. They buried their dead, revered their ancestors and had complex religious beliefs and ceremonies centring on worship of a Creator and respect for all living things.

Making a Living

In addition to hunting, warfare and trading were important activities for the early Indians. Some were peaceful, while others were often at war with their neighbours. They all traded to some extent with their neighbours, and some made long trading expeditions. The Assiniboine of the southern prairies, for example, made month-long journeys in late summer to the Missouri Valley to trade beads and hides for corn. Tobacco, obtained through trade from the east, was popular, and pieces of copper and Pacific coast shells have been found at archaeological sites.

Indians living in most of Saskatchewan relied heavily on the buffalo for food, but they made use of the animal for many other purposes as well. Hides became clothing, blankets and lodge coverings. Bones were used as tools, sinew as string, bone marrow and fat in the making of pemmican — a highly nutritious mixture of dried meat and berries that could last for months without spoiling. Even dried buffalo dung was used as fuel for fires.

Most often, hunters went out in groups, and the catch from a successful hunt could last a band a whole season. The buffalo would be driven into pounds, or corrals, where they could be easily killed, or over cliffs called jumps. At some pound and jump sites, drive lines — rocks used to mark a funnel-shaped path the buffalo were driven along — can still be seen.

Although the buffalo was the chief source of food and other necessities, Saskatchewan Indians also hunted mule deer, elk, moose and pronghorn. The Dene of the north relied primarily on the caribou. Hunters also snared smaller animals, such as rabbits, squirrels and beaver, gathered birds' eggs and caught fish.

Buffalo hunting became much easier for the Plains Indians after horses reached the Canadian prairies in the mid-1700s.

Although Saskatchewan Indians didn't practise agriculture, they had many vegetables in their diet. One of the most common was the breadroot, a prairie plant with a large underground tuber, much like a potato. Other wild plants eaten included wild rice, prairie onion, cattails, berries, rosehips, acorns, hazelnuts, roots and greens. Indians also used a variety of flowers, herbs and grasses for medicinal and ceremonial purposes.

Making a living in both historic and prehistoric times meant mobility for the Indians — going to where the food and other resources were. Indian bands followed the buffalo or the caribou herds, and they travelled to areas where certain plants grew in the summer, and to sheltered areas like wooded valleys in the winter.

Life for Indians in Saskatchewan was difficult, but they were efficient hunters and gatherers, and they adapted to changing natural conditions. They developed skills and a knowledge of their environment that enabled them to live comfortably, except at times when disasters such as floods or drought made animals scarce and there was famine.

As buffalo became more numerous, so did the human population. Weapons, hunting techniques and other technology slowly changed. Earliest weapons were long, large-headed lances. Later, smaller spears or darts were used with a throwing stick, or *atlatl,* that allowed spears to be hurled 30 metres (100 feet) with accuracy and force. Pottery was first used about 2000 years ago. The bow and arrow, which made hunting easier and safer, developed about 500 years later. People became less migratory.

The band was the basic unit of political organization for Plains Indians, with a group of bands making up a nation and a number of nations sometimes further organized into a confederacy. Rivalries and alliances between nations and confederacies caused warfare but also led to trade. Over the years, territorial patterns changed. The Cree of Ontario, for example, spread to the western woodlands and eventually to the plains, becoming the largest group in Saskatchewan. The Gros Ventre moved south to Montana and the Blackfoot went west into Alberta. The introduction of guns and horses, around 1750, had a major impact on these patterns.

In Pursuit of the Beaver

The modern history of the area that is now known as Saskatchewan, like that of its neighbours to the east and west, begins with a craze that raged across Europe for beaver hats.

For western Canada, the fur trading story began in earnest in 1670. That year, England's King Charles II granted title to a vast area of the New World to a group of businessmen who called themselves the "Company of Adventurers of England Trading into Hudson's Bay," soon more commonly referred to simply as the Hudson's Bay Company. Including as it did all the lands that drained into Hudson Bay, Rupert's Land — named after Prince Rupert, the king's cousin — was an incredibly rich chunk of real estate. All the Company was

The Plains Indians welcomed Henry Kelsey when he reached their lands in the spring of 1691. They allowed him to stay with them, learn their ways, take part in buffalo hunts. But they did not accept his invitation to become part of the Hudson's Bay Company fur-trading network.

interested in, however, was furs. The Adventurers built a fort called York Factory on the southwestern shore of the Bay and went into business buying furs from the Indians, who were more than happy to exchange such everyday items for metal tools, cooking utensils, guns and cloth.

For a time the Company men had the northwestern trade pretty much to themselves. Then, in the 1730s, a French Canadian named La Vérendrye followed the St. Lawrence-Great Lakes route into the interior and headed west from Lake Superior, establishing posts at strategic locations as he went. He reached the South Saskatchewan River in 1741, and his sons trekked north from there and built Fort Paskoyac on the Carrot River a few years later. These posts did not at first represent a very serious threat to the Hudson's Bay Company, but after Britain took possession of New France in 1763, the situation changed. Newly established Montreal merchants began sending traders out to operate along the old French route and establish new posts. The Company retaliated in 1774 by sending Samuel Hearne to build Cumberland House on the Saskatchewan River, just west of what is now the Manitoba border. It was the first permanent European settlement in the area.

Eventually, some of the Montreal-based traders, scornfully referred to as "Pedlars" by their rivals because they went directly to Indian encampments to trade, began to co-ordinate their efforts. A group of them came together to form the North West Company, and competition between the new company and the old became fierce. Finally, in 1821, with the winds of change blowing into the West, they merged into one, retaining the Hudson's Bay name.

A Way of Life Ends — and a New One Begins

During the early years of the fur trade, the rhythms of Native life remained relatively unchanged. Indians became indispensable to the European traders as suppliers and middlemen, and their societies and culture were basically unaffected.

The Cree and Assiniboine excelled as middlemen in the trade, buying and selling with more distant groups, or charging tolls to those who travelled through their territory to Hudson Bay. Along with the Saulteaux in Manitoba and the Blackfoot in Alberta, the Cree and Assiniboine controlled the western interior. Their power increased, their lives were made easier by trade goods, their societies were enriched rather than disrupted.

However, during the period of western expansion of the trade marked by the aggressive Pedlars, the role of the Indians changed: fewer were needed as middlemen, more as suppliers, not only of pelts but also of pemmican. And, gradually, conditions changed as they became more dependent on European trade goods: guns, knives, axes, cooking utensils, cloth, tobacco and, all the worse for them, alcohol. More energy was expended on gathering furs to trade than on providing for their own needs in traditional ways. As well, European diseases such as measles and smallpox killed many Indians, who had no immunity to them.

Still, as long as European interest in the West remained focused on furs, the Native people of the area fared relatively well. As soon as European eyes began to look at land, however, Indians were in dire trouble. The great disaster came for the peoples of the Plains in the late 1870s: within an incredibly few years, the great buffalo herds, heedlessly shot in the millions for the price their tongue would bring, dwindled then totally disappeared from the Prairies. Powerless to stop the rising tide of white expansion and left without any means of supporting themselves adequately, the Indians had little choice but to move onto reserves the federal government had set aside for them.

The years that followed were a dark time for Saskatchewan's Indians. The government was convinced that their best hope was to settle down to farming their reserves, learn English and adopt the ways of the new majority. To that end, it took control of virtually every aspect of their lives and took over the education of their children, discouraging the use of their own languages and

The North Battleford Powwow is one of many held across the province every summer.

customs. Over the years, many individuals overcame the difficulties they faced and made a success of their lives. But in general, the result was a vicious circle of poverty, alcohol and discrimination.

Only in recent years has there been a resurgence of pride among Saskatchewan Indians and a new determination to survive on their own terms. Political groups such as the Federation of Saskatchewan Indian Nations and the Métis Society of Saskatchewan have been formed, and the creation of institutions such as the Saskatchewan Indian Federated College in Regina gives hope for better times ahead. This reassertion of the province's Indian and Métis peoples reached a new stage in 1992 with a settlement on land claims, worth about $340 million, and talks aimed at Native self-government. More recently, Natives have entered into a partnership with the provincial government to operate casino gambling, on and off reserves.

CHAPTER 5
The Northwest Rebellion

Saskatchewan was slow to be settled. In fact, it was not until almost 200 years after Henry Kelsey's visit that Europeans in any great number began to move to what was then being called both "The Great Lone Land" and "The Last Best West."

Catholic missionaries had first arrived in the West in 1743, with the Church of England quickly following, and several missions and church-run schools were operating in the West by the middle of the nineteenth century. Travellers began to come through the area, and two scientific journeys paved the way for the developments to come: Captain John Palliser's expedition, sent by the British government in the mid-1850s, and that of Henry Hind, sent soon afterwards by Canadian authorities.

Palliser identified a fertile parkland belt roughly following the Qu'Appelle and South and North Saskatchewan rivers, and an unsuitable semi-arid "triangle" that encompassed almost all of the southern Saskatchewan prairie. Hind was more optimistic, including a large part of the prairie in his fertile belt projection.

Canada Takes Over

In the years immediately following Confederation, great and rapid transformations came to the West.

In 1869, the Dominion of Canada made arrangements to purchase all of Rupert's Land, including most of present-day Saskatchewan, from the Hudson's Bay Company. After some delays caused by

The Battle of Fish Creek, April 23, 1885

Holy Trinity Anglican Church at Stanley Mission on the Churchill River is the oldest building still standing in Saskatchewan. It was built between 1854 and 1860 from local logs and stained glass brought from England.

Métis opposition in the Red River area, the Dominion took control in 1870. A tiny part of its vast new possession became the province of Manitoba; the rest was called the North-West Territories and would be administered from Ottawa.

One of Prime Minister John A. Macdonald's great fears was that the United States would move in and take over the Canadian West unless Canada quickly established a strong presence there. He therefore proceeded to take all possible measures to do just that.

By 1871, surveyors were busy dividing the land into townships and the townships into 259-hectare (640-acre) sections, and quarter-sections. That same year a railway across the West was promised as a condition of British Columbia's entry into Confederation. In 1872 the Dominion Lands Act was passed offering settlers a quarter-section for little more than a promise to build a house and farm a specified amount of it within three years. The following year the murder of a group of Assiniboine by drunken American wolf hunters (an incident that came to be known as the Cypress Hill Massacre) spurred the formation of the

"Crossing the Dirt Hills," by journalist Henri Julien, who accompanied the Mounted Police on their long march west. The march began south of Winnipeg on July 8, 1874, and was much tougher than anyone had expected. By the time the expedition reached the Dirt Hills a month later, the horses were so weakened by the heat and lack of water and feed that the men had to get down and help pull the wagons and guns.

North-West Mounted Police (NWMP). The first contingent arrived in 1874.

Parliament passed the North-West Territories Act in 1875, forming the basis for local government, and Battleford, on the North Saskatchewan River, was selected as capital. Postal and telegraph systems were established, making communication considerably easier and faster. And finally, after many delays due to political scandal and lack of funds, the railway reached Regina in 1882.

In the meantime, the disappearance of the buffalo left the Plains Indians in a desperate situation. This made it easier for the government to make treaties with them and restrict them to reserves. The brutal Indian wars which characterized the settling of the American West were, therefore, avoided in Canada.

Early Settlement

While people didn't exactly pour into Saskatchewan during this period, they were coming in increasing numbers. The troubles involved in the creation of Manitoba in 1870 brought many Red River Métis, who settled mainly in the Batoche-St. Laurent area on the South Saskatchewan River, south of Prince Albert. There were also several small communities of English-speaking farmers who had come from Ontario and Britain. Most of these settlements were in the parkland or in hilly areas just to the south, while the prairie was still largely empty.

Various schemes were designed to promote settlement, and organizations and companies were given incentives to bring in immigrants. Colonies were formed, including several sponsored by British aristocrats. The best known was probably Cannington Manor,

The trek to the new homestead. *Inset:* Sod cabin. In the south, where wood was scarce, settlers often built their first house of sod "bricks." The great advantage of sod was that it was free. The great disadvantage was that a sod roof absorbed water and leaked for days after a rain.

in the Moose Mountain area, which attracted wealthy young Englishmen, many of whom spent almost as much time fox hunting, racing horses and playing polo and tennis as they did farming.

It had been expected that the railway would follow Palliser's "fertile belt" northwest from Winnipeg. An alternative, cheaper route due west, across the prairies, was finally chosen, however. This decision was partly the result of a third study of the area by botanist John Macoun, who predicted that much of the Palliser Triangle would actually be ideal wheat land.

As the Canadian Pacific Railway (CPR) pushed its way across the prairie, towns sprang up almost overnight: Regina, Moose Jaw, Swift Current, Maple Creek and others. Communities in the north, such as Battleford and Prince Albert, previously the focus of attention, began to feel alienated and dissatisfied. They were especially offended when, in 1883, the capital was moved to Regina, then a tiny village described by the *Manitoba Free Press* as being "in the midst of a vast plain of inferior soil...with about enough water in the miserable little creek...to wash a sheep."

Western Grievances

The grievances of three groups began to come together in 1884.

The 1500 or so Métis living in the Batoche area had been impoverished by the end of the buffalo hunt and the effects of the railway and steamboats on the freighting business they carried on with their famous Red River carts. Now they were beset by fears of the changes the influx of new, mostly British, settlers would bring and concerns over title to the lands they had settled.

At the same time, Indians were having a difficult time adjusting to life on reserves. The financially pressed federal government had begun undermining rights guaranteed by the treaties and even cut back on food rations. There was mass hunger in many areas, and some of the chiefs, led by Big Bear, were attempting to forge unity among the tribes with an eye to rewriting the treaties. As Chief Poundmaker observed, the whites had promised everything but delivered only hunger, disease and death.

Even white settlers were angry at Ottawa. In Prince Albert and Battleford, they were bitter about being bypassed by the railway, about high transportation costs, about the government's failure to create conditions that would bring prosperity.

Violence Erupts

Into this highly charged environment stepped Louis Riel. A fiery young leader of the Métis in Manitoba, Riel had fled following the trouble there and was working as a teacher in Montana. He was older now, but he hadn't lost his dream of a Métis nation. When approached by a group of Métis and white settlers led by Gabriel Dumont, he was more than ready to resume his role as leader.

At this point there was no thought of rebellion. Making Batoche his headquarters, Riel began speaking to people, gathering support and sending off letters to Ottawa. Eventually, a petition was sent asking for local government. When there was no reaction, Riel grew pessimistic and began to talk more and more wildly. As tensions rose, the Catholic Church, alarmed at the threat of violence, withdrew the support it had at first given him. White settlers also began to distance themselves from the Métis, and the Indians were undecided which way to go. The coalition they had hoped to forge now shattered, Riel and the Métis decided to go it on their own. Riel declared a provisional government on March 19, 1885. Ottawa at last announced a commission to investigate Métis land claims, but it was too little too late.

The first clash occurred at Duck Lake on March 26, 1885, when Superintendent L.W.F. Crozier of the NWMP led a force of about a hundred policemen and volunteers against Dumont, the Métis military leader, and his men. The battle lasted only half an hour, but it left 12 dead and 11 wounded among the police and 5 dead on the

Métis side. The rout of the police would have been worse, but Riel stopped Dumont from pursuing Crozier and his fleeing men.

As a result of this humiliating defeat — their first ever — the NWMP lost face and there was a breakdown of law and order across the West. Hungry Indians looted stores and homesteads in isolated incidents; on April 2, members of Big Bear's band got out of control at the tiny Hudson's Bay post at Frog Lake, just west of what is now the border between Saskatchewan and Alberta, and killed nine white men. Ten days later, emboldened by Frog Lake, they laid siege to Fort Pitt, on the Saskatchewan side. NWMP Inspector Francis Dickens (son of the famous English writer Charles Dickens) surrendered the fort and fled with his men. Several white civilians were taken prisoner by the Cree under Big Bear's protection and the fort was burned.

News of the looting and the Frog Lake killings sparked fears of a general Indian uprising. In fact, despite the sensational publicity in the East over these incidents, most Indian leaders were urging restraint and acts of violence by Indians were few and isolated.

The Government Responds

Ottawa responded by sending out a call for volunteers for a military force. Thousands of militia were soon headed west by rail.

Major General Frederick Dobson Middleton, the commander of the Canadian Militia, was already in the West, and on the morning of April 6, he and 800 men marched north from Qu'Appelle, near Regina. At Batoche, 350 Métis and Indians, only about 200 of them armed, awaited them. Dumont, who had fought against the Sioux in Montana, wanted to wage hit-and-run guerrilla-style attacks against the Canadian troops at night, but was held back by Riel. With Middleton's troops practically in sight, Riel finally gave his blessing and, on April 23, Dumont set up an ambush at Fish Creek, with 200 to 300 Métis and Indians.

Fortunately for the government troops, the Métis began firing too early and the ambush failed. The day-long battle ended in stalemate, but the rebels, who lost over 50 horses and used up much of their scarce ammunition, were badly shaken by their first encounter with artillery. The Métis sent pleas to Big Bear and Poundmaker for help — they refused — and dug in at Batoche. Middleton fell back and sent for more equipment and men.

On May 7, Middleton marched to Batoche with 850 men and a Gatling gun, the latest in military hardware. An attempt at a co-ordinated land-water attack went almost comically awry when the steamboat *Northcote*, drifting down the river, ran into a trap set by Dumont: a steel ferry cable strung across the river, which neatly chopped off the steamship's smokestack, disabling it.

The fight raged for three days. On the morning of the fourth day, with the Métis down to duck shot and pellets made from melted

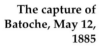
The capture of Batoche, May 12, 1885

nails, two officers deliberately misunderstood an order from the ever-cautious Middleton and advanced on the rebels, who fled. At least six Métis were killed in the final furious battle, including a 93-year-old man. Dumont wanted to carry on with guerrilla war, but Riel felt it was God's will for the rebellion to fail and on May 15 he surrendered. Dumont fled to Montana.

There were two other significant battles to the rebellion. A force of some 500 men under Colonel William Otter had been sent to relieve Battleford, where hundreds of people had sought shelter in the fort. On May 1, Otter and 300 men marched on to Cut Knife Hill, where they clashed with a force of 200 Cree and Stoneys led by

After their victory at Cut Knife Hill, Poundmaker and his men moved towards Batoche to help the Métis. But they took too long — the battle was over before they arrived. Realizing that further resistance was useless, Poundmaker surrendered to General Middleton on May 26.

Poundmaker. By noon the next day, they were retreating with heavy casualties. Once again, the soldiers were lucky — Poundmaker let them go, and stopped his men from pursuing them. The final act in the drama was played in late May when a large militia force took on Big Bear's band at Frenchman's Butte and Loon Lake. After a brief fight the Cree fled. For five weeks, Big Bear managed to elude a massive manhunt, then surrendered at Fort Carlton on July 2. A NWMP officer remarked sourly that Big Bear had given himself up to the only men in the territories who weren't out looking for him.

The rebellion was over.

Aftermath

In all, an 8000-man force had been raised by Ottawa and $5 million spent to deal with several hundred poorly armed Métis and a thousand or so starving Indians. Twenty-six soldiers and a dozen policemen had been killed and over a hundred wounded. Of the rebels, 72 were dead, 191 wounded. A few civilians were killed.

Over a hundred rebels — 46 Métis and 81 Indians — were brought to trial, mostly for treason; 7 Métis were convicted and so were 44 Indians, including 8 hanged for murder. Two white men charged with complicity were acquitted. Big Bear and Poundmaker were both jailed for their part in the fighting they had tried to prevent. They came out of prison broken and died soon afterwards.

Riel's trial in Regina was front page news across the nation. He was convicted of treason, though the all-white, Protestant jury recommended leniency, citing the legitimate grievances of the Métis. Quebec clamoured for a reprieve, but Macdonald wouldn't relent. Riel was hanged in Regina on November 16, 1885.

By then, of course, the Métis were broken. Many of them scattered across the West and to the U.S. Some were awarded land — about 2200 hectares (55 000 acres) in all — by the commission set up as the rebellion began, but many were cheated out of it by speculators.

The Indians returned to their reserves, demoralized, finished as a

The trial of Louis Riel. Riel's lawyers tried to prove he was insane, and therefore not guilty. Riel himself, however, fiercely insisted on his sanity; the jury took him at his word and found him guilty.

military force, their diplomatic efforts at Native unity and their hopes of winning better treaty terms smashed.

The rebellion had brought national attention to the West and Ottawa's quick action in putting it down paved the way for further settlement. It was truly the end of an era.

A Footnote to History

Riel's story has been a source of controversy in Canadian history ever since. In Quebec, he was hailed as a hero, and the Métis community in the West has long campaigned to have his name cleared. In Regina, a plaque commemorating his trial and execution stands in downtown Victoria Park, just across the street from where the courthouse once stood. A play re-enacting the trial is performed every summer, and a sympathetic biography by Regina author Maggie Siggins further enchances Riel's reputation.

In March 1992, the federal government recognized "the unique and historic role" of Riel as a founder of Manitoba and "his contribution in the development of Confederation."

CHAPTER 6
The Last Best West

Life on the prairies was harsh for settlers. They were isolated. The nearest neighbour might be two or three hours away by horse and buggy, the nearest community even farther. The elements were merciless — howling blizzards in winter, blistering heat in summer, grass fires that spread unbelievably fast — and so were the mosquitoes and black flies. Dwellings were crude shacks made of sod where wood was scarce, or of logs where trees were available. There was no power or phone, doctors were few and usually beyond reach in any emergency. Farm families could raise animals for meat and grow their own vegetables, gather berries and nuts in the summer, even mill their own flour. But they had little cash to buy the other necessities of life, much less any of its comforts. As distant as neighbours might be, they were precious, and helping one another out became a way of life.

In the decade following the rebellion, immigration continued at a slow but steady pace. Swedes settled in the Qu'Appelle Valley in 1887, calling their community New Stockholm. Other Scandinavians followed: Norwegians and Finns in the park belt, Icelanders at Thingvalla and Foam Lake, Danes in New Denmark. Hungarians settled in Esterhazy, named after a count who sponsored them. Romanians came to the Regina area. German communities were begun in Balgonie and Ebenezer, and Jewish settlers came to Oxbow and Edenbridge (where the Beth Israel Synagogue, oldest in the province, still stands). Ukrainians arrived in the Yorkton area in 1897.

Richardson, a typical farm town on the CPR line southeast of Regina

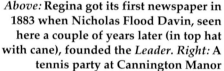
Above: Regina got its first newspaper in 1883 when Nicholas Flood Davin, seen here a couple of years later (in top hat with cane), founded the *Leader. Right:* A tennis party at Cannington Manor

Political reforms, sparked by the rebellion, brought four seats in Parliament and two in the Senate to the Territories. In 1888, Ottawa passed a law establishing a territorial assembly of 22 elected members with the power to levy taxes. F.W.G. Haultain, an Ontarian who had gone west to practise law, soon became head of the Executive Council and the guiding hand leading the Territories toward provincehood.

With all these developments, the Territories began to take on the clatter and hum of Canadian life, even though people were still relatively few and far between. A typical village of the day would contain a general store, post office, blacksmith shop, livery stable, hotel, café, railway station, perhaps a school. Although the settlers worked hard, there was time for play: curling, horse races, fairs, football and lacrosse, cricket and tennis among the British, even fox hunting in some areas, were all popular. Towns along the CPR boasted a variety of cultural pursuits. Regina in 1891 had a town hall for lectures, plays and concerts. It had banks, insurance agents, doctors and lawyers, brick and stone houses — even electricity and telephone. In 1895, it hosted a large territorial fair. A wooden plank sidewalk was built linking the fair grounds to downtown Albert Street, as Regina's sticky gumbo soil made walking almost impossible when it rained. Machinery and livestock were displayed and there was entertainment to suit every taste, including band concerts and a beauty pageant.

Searching for Immigrants

The 1896 federal election brought the Liberals under Wilfrid Laurier to power in Ottawa. The new government like the old saw the West as a potential agricultural heartland, producing food for an industrialized East and a market for its manufactured goods. The new Minister of the Interior was Manitoba lawyer Clifford Sifton. It was his responsibility to get the West settled and he tackled the job with vigour and imagination.

Up to now efforts to attract settlers had been directed mainly at Britain and the United States. But what Sifton really wanted was farmers, and it soon became clear to him that those traditional sources of immigration were not producing enough of them fast enough. He therefore redirected his department's advertising efforts towards first Western, then Central and Eastern Europeans. He simplified regulations, opened up new lands for homesteading and began to blanket Europe with pamphlets in over a dozen different languages. The results were all he could have hoped for, and the trickle of immigrants became a flood.

Large numbers of Hungarians, Germans and Ukrainians now came. There were a number of Mennonite communities, and a group of 7400 Doukhobours, fleeing from religious persecution in Russia, arrived at Yorkton in 1899. Britons continued to come as well, individually and in groups. A group of 400 Spanish-speaking Welsh, who had earlier migrated to Patagonia in South America, settled in the Saltcoats area. There were also new arrivals from Ontario, and a group of French-Canadians from Quebec settled at

Above: **Barr colonists camped out at Saskatoon in 1903. Recruited in England by Rev. Isaac Barr, the 2000 settlers had a harrowing journey: baggage lost, trains missed, expected supplies and accommodation nowhere to be found. Another Anglican clergyman, Rev. G. E. Lloyd took over as leader in Saskatoon and finally got the colonists to their homesteads. In gratitude, they named their settlement Lloydminster.** *Left:* **Polish mother and child at Sheho**

Gravelbourg in 1906. Southern Saskatchewan became a checkerboard of settlements, many of them with their own language and culture.

At the same time, the Indian population was decreasing, as a result of tuberculosis, a change of diet and demoralization. Some 300 000 hectares (750 000 acres) of treaty land was taken back and made available to settlers.

In 1901, Premier Haultain formally began requests that the Territories be made a province. He wanted one large one. Others wanted two. Laurier decided on two, and laws creating Alberta and Saskatchewan were passed by Parliament on July 5, 1905.

The Making of a Province

With appropriate fanfare and celebration, Saskatchewan became a province on September 1, 1905.

No one deserved to be premier of Saskatchewan more than Haultain, but he had made the error of backing the Conservatives in the previous federal election, and Laurier gave the job to Thomas Walter Scott. A newspaperman who had served in Parliament, Scott became leader of the provincial Liberals just days before taking over as premier. The first provincial election held later that year confirmed him in office, and it was thus his hand on the wheel as Saskatchewan raced into the twentieth century. Scott remained premier for 11 years, and the party stayed in power, with just a five-year break, until the closing days of the Second World War.

Immigrants continued to flood into the new province. Over 20 000 homesteads were registered in 1905 alone. There was, however, a change in the pattern of immigration. Frank Oliver, who replaced Sifton as interior minister that year, considered his predecessor's policies too open. He shifted the focus of his advertising efforts back to Britain and the U.S., in hopes of preserving the "national fabric" of Canada. Partly as a result, and partly because the American West was now settled and land there had become expensive, the largest group of immigrants in the period that followed were Americans, around 50 000 of them.

By the turn of the century, it had become clear that the CPR was having trouble meeting the needs of the growing population. In response to the demand for better service, a new transcontinental rail line, the Canadian Northern, was built, crossing Saskatchewan's park belt in 1903-04. It was soon joined by another, the Grand Trunk Pacific, built just a little to the south. Grain elevators were put up at regular intervals and villages quickly sprang up around them. Every town had a Chinese café, serving meals for 25 cents. Operating a restaurant was one of the few

A fairly low-key government poster. Some of the posters and pamphlets painted such a glowing picture of the Canadian West that immigrants were disappointed in what they found. Commented one: "The kindest thing to say is that the literature was on the optimistic side."

occupations open to Chinese workers who had helped build the CPR, but who were discriminated against and denied citizenship.

As the province blossomed, so did its capital city. Its population had climbed to 30 000 by 1911, and its impressive Legislative Building was completed the following year. That same year, however, on June 30, Regina was hit by a devastating cyclone that killed 28 people, injured over 200 and left 2500 homeless. In three terrifying minutes, hundreds of buildings were destroyed. But such was the optimism and spirit of the community that rebuilding began immediately. "Nothing — mark the word nothing — can check Regina's progress....The new Regina...will far outrival the Regina that was so badly stricken," crowed the *Leader*.

Above: **Aftermath of the cyclone that devastated Regina in 1912.** *Left:* **Prince Albert tailor shop**

Wheat Is King

By 1905, agriculture had already become firmly entrenched as the primary focus of the new province. Developments came quickly, spurred by the demands of dryland farming. New types of wheat, fall ploughing and the use of summerfallowing — letting fields "rest" for a season — all improved yields. The mechanical reaper replaced the sickle and scythe, followed by the mower, binder, thresher and seed drill, all powered at first by oxen or horses.

The farmers' job was growing grain, and they did it fairly well. But grain storage, transportation and distribution were in other hands and often caused problems for farmers. The Saskatchewan Grain Growers Association (SGGA) became a powerful voice, and a constant thorn in the side of governments. As a result of the SGGA's efforts, a system of hail insurance was developed, a co-operative elevator company was formed, and government financial assistance was obtained for railway branch lines, making transportation of grain cheaper and easier.

The 1914 crop was poor, due to drought and an early frost, underscoring warnings that farmers needed to diversify. But a bonanza 1915 crop, and a growing clamour for wheat to help feed war-torn Europe, set that idea back. Saskatchewan became even more dependent on wheat in the following years.

The federal government took control of wheat sales during the war but gave it up afterwards, angering farmers, who were already upset over a number of other issues: freight rates, tariffs, debt, recession. Saskatchewan farmers were not alone in their discontent: a "farmer's revolt" led to the creation of farmer political parties that won power in Alberta, Ontario and Manitoba. But in Saskatchewan the Liberals, who had always had good relations with farmers, were able to absorb the movement.

Unhappiness with federal farm policies led to the rise of the Farmers' Union of Canada, which gained strength in Saskatchewan at the expense of the SGGA. The two joined forces in 1923, however, to form the Saskatchewan Wheat Pool, giving a further push to the co-operative movement. The Pool is now the largest grain handler in the world and Canada's largest co-op. It's also the largest business in Saskatchewan.

The War Years

War broke out in Europe in the summer of 1914, bringing mixed feelings to Saskatchewan. Those of British origin were eager to fight, as were many European immigrants whose countries were caught up on the allied side in the war. But settlers from Germany, Austria and other countries that were fighting on the other side tried to keep a low profile. They were mistrusted, as were the Doukhobours and Mennonites for their pacifism. Some lost the right to vote, and many who were of military age were placed in internment camps.

About 42 000 Saskatchewan men served their country during the war. Saskatchewan units suffered 17 594 casualties, including 4385 deaths. At home, an epidemic of Spanish flu killed as many Saskatchewan people as the war did.

Social Reform

During the years leading up to the war, a "social gospel" led by some of the Protestant churches swept North America. Its advocates preached that churches should devote themselves to solving social problems such as poverty, illiteracy and crime. Associated with it was the Temperance movement against alcohol and the push for women's rights — the Suffrage movement. Both movements were popular in Saskatchewan.

The Grain Growers Association had supported women's suffrage as early as 1912, with Violet McNaughton, the head of its women's section, a vocal champion of the movement. Suffragists collected 11 000 names on a petition calling for the vote for women and presented it to the government in 1915. The government finally acted on February 14, 1916, just two weeks after Manitoba led the way. The following year, another bill was passed allowing women to hold office. Two years later Sarah Ramsland, a Liberal, became the first woman elected to the legislature.

Premier Scott hesitated on prohibition, the goal of the Temperance movement, but in 1915, the government closed bars and took over the retail sale of liquor. At the end of 1916, the province became officially "dry." After the war, support for prohibition waned, and for a brief period, liquor from Saskatchewan found a ready market in the "dry" United States.

Rum-running was big business, particularly close to the border, and the RCMP estimated in 1923 that there were "more illicit stills in Saskatchewan...than in all the rest of Canada."

There was a dark side to the social reform movement as well as a progressive one. Its message focused to a large extent on the deplorable conditions in which most European immigrants lived in Western cities. During the war years and afterwards, that message was sometimes distorted into a false patriotism and prejudice against "foreigners," who, by this time, made up a large part of the Saskatchewan population. Tensions over language and religion, often centring on the schools, increased. The arrival of the Ku Klux Klan in the 1920s crystallized existing biases against Catholics and foreigners. Some prominent Saskatchewanians joined, and the first public Klan gathering in Canada was held in Moose Jaw in the spring of 1927. Interest soon waned, however.

Along with social developments, there were technological

Regina had Canada's first registered "Air Harbour," seen here in 1920.

changes. The telephone had a tremendous effect on easing the isolation of pioneer life. So too did radio, which brought the outside world to Saskatchewan, and the automobile, which dramatically shrank distances and removed much of the hardship of rural life. Movies became the rage, and the Chautauqua circuit of plays, concerts and comedy was popular. So were slot machines, briefly. The gasoline engine replaced steam and, finally, ox and horse as agriculture became completely mechanized.

The Dirty Thirties

Although it ended almost sixty years ago, the Great Depression still looms large in the imagination of the people of Saskatchewan. Nowhere were the effects of the economic crash of 1929 and the lean years that followed worse than in Saskatchewan, where the situation was complicated by a severe drought. Not only did the price of wheat take a nose dive, but very little of it was grown. What was grown was attacked by plagues of grasshoppers.

Wheat prices, which had been $1.60 a bushel in 1929, dropped below 40 cents in 1933. Saskatchewan plummeted from fourth-wealthiest province to poorest. And, as the drought dragged on, things actually worsened, reaching their lowest point in 1937 and 1938. Drought turned much of the Grain Belt into a desert, just as

During the drought of the 1930s, prairie topsoil was as dry and loose as desert sand.

Regina, Dominion Day 1935. A meeting of relief camp strikers and their sympathizers turns into a riot when police try to arrest their leaders.

Palliser had predicted. Farmland was ravaged by erosion, fields were stripped of topsoil. Dust storms were so thick they turned the sky black. It wasn't for nothing that Saskatchewan farmers coined the expression "Dirty Thirties."

Some people quit farming and headed for the cities — or for the hobo jungles that lined the railway tracks. Others became totally dependent on government relief and charity. Hundreds of boxcars of fruit, vegetables and clothing were donated by people in Ontario and shipped to Saskatchewan. Farmers took the engines out of their cars and hooked them up to horses, calling them Bennett Buggies, after R.B. Bennett, the Conservative prime minister.

With all this heartache, tempers grew short.

In September 1931, striking coal miners in Estevan defied a ban to stage a parade that ended in a confrontation with the police. Three strikers were killed and 23 injured along with a number of policemen.

But the worst trouble in the country came in 1935 and is remembered as the Regina Riot. With so many unemployed, many single men wound up in work camps. About 1000 of them from camps on the West Coast decided to march on Ottawa. They headed east on CPR freight trains, picking up support and numbers along the way. By the time they reached Regina, their numbers had doubled. On July 1, many of the On-to-Ottawa Trekkers attended a fund-raising rally downtown in Victoria Park, along with hundreds of sympathetic local residents and farmers from surrounding areas. Everything was peaceful until the RCMP and Regina police attempted to arrest the trek leaders. This touched off a brawl in which one policeman was killed, and 43 policemen and 39 civilians were injured.

Once More to War

Saskatchewan had a few more years of drought and depression to survive, and somehow it did. The rains came back after 1937, and the Second World War, which began in 1939, swept away the last traces of the Depression. A Saskatchewan-born soldier, General Andrew McNaughton, was commander of Canadian forces overseas, including over 70 000 men and women from his home province. Saskatchewan pilots flew in the Battle of Britain and many farm boys from the province took part in the doomed defence of Hong Kong in 1941. Others were in the invasion of Sicily and Italy, and the D-Day invasion of France. They were also part of the force that liberated Holland and pressed into Germany.

The British Commonwealth Air Training Plan (BCATP) brought thousands of pilots and ground crew from Britain and other Commonwealth countries to Canada for training. Fifteen military bases were built in Saskatchewan, including one at Moose Jaw, where a large base still exists. By the end of the war, Saskatchewan had trained a fifth of the BCATP pilots, and up to a third of some categories of air crew.

The war had an immediate effect on the unemployment of the previous decade, replacing it with shortages of farm labour. The price of wheat rose, and there was a demand for other crops and livestock. Saskatchewan agriculture finally began the diversification that had been sidetracked by the First World War.

CHAPTER 7

The CCF Years
to the Present

The postwar history of Saskatchewan really began before the war had even ended. Tommy Douglas, who would become the province's most popular premier ever, led the left-wing Co-operative Commonwealth Federation (CCF) to victory in the 1944 election and ushered in a new era.

No one in Canada loves politics more than the residents of Saskatchewan, and they have been enthusiastic participants in a fascinating struggle for the past 50 years. The social and economic life of the province during that period has been marked by the erosion of the rural way of life and attempts to diversify the economy. The struggle against the former and for the latter was the backdrop against which has been played out a political contest between "socialism" and "free enterprise."

The CCF Agenda

The CCF was born in Calgary in 1932 out of an alliance between a radical group of farmers and unionists. It had its baptism the following year at a meeting in Regina. That meeting produced the famous Regina Manifesto, which promised to end capitalism and establish socialism. The ravages of the Depression had convinced reformers that the system needed to be radically altered.

During the CCF's 20 years in power, government services expanded dramatically. Labour laws were liberalized and price support for farmers was introduced. Attention was given to

Canada Day fireworks at Wascana Centre, Regina

developing the north and its resources. Thousands of kilometres of new road were built. Free medical and dental service was provided to pensioners immediately, and in 1947 the Saskatchewan Hospitalization Plan, the grandparent of today's national Medicare system, began providing hospital coverage at $5 per person. It was so popular the Opposition didn't dare criticize it.

The CCF experimented with Crown corporations, establishing government-owned companies of all types, from one providing automobile insurance to a brick works, a woollen mill and a tannery. The government bought out a box factory and a shoe factory, even a small airline. Saskatchewan then became the first province to use planes and parachutes in fighting forest fires and established the first air ambulance service in the world.

With the memory of the Dirty Thirties still fresh, the Douglas government tried to create a Depression-proof economy.

Social programs cost money, of course, and the government's economic situation was complicated by the fact that it had inherited

Tommy Douglas (centre), the leader of the Saskatchewan CCF, inspects one of his party's campaign billboards in 1944.

a debt of $180 million, more than four times the size of its annual budget. Fortunately, Saskatchewan's rich natural resources were about to start paying off. Uranium was discovered in 1950, and the federal government's Eldorado mining company began production two years later. The Leduc oil strike in Alberta in 1947 set off exploration in Saskatchewan as well, with numerous finds of both oil and gas. Rich deposits of salt and potash were found beneath the prairies. Over the next few years, these industries were rapidly adding to the wealth of the province.

The Battle Over Medicare

In the early sixties, just as Tommy Douglas left Saskatchewan politics to become the national leader of the newly formed New Democratic

Anti-Medicare demonstrators hang Premier Woodrow Lloyd in effigy outside the Legislative Building during the 1962 doctors' strike.

Party (NDP), the government prepared to press ahead with its plan for a universal medical insurance scheme. The Medicare program was introduced in the Legislature in late 1961, with July 1, 1962, as the proposed starting date. The Liberals opposed it, but they couldn't stop it. The province's doctors were determined to fight it all the way.

The government offered some concessions to the doctors, but they wouldn't budge. Tensions rose and rumours spread that many doctors were planning to move to the U.S. The province became polarized. Citizens formed committees in support of Medicare; others rallied behind banners reading "Keep our doctors" in support of the medical profession. On July 1, doctors went on strike. Hospitals operated on emergency basis only. The government recruited British doctors and set up community clinics. Finally, a mediator brought the two sides together, and the strike ended July 23. Doctors at first worked grudgingly under the plan, but within a year it appeared to be a complete success.

The Thatcher Years

It was a somewhat weakened CCF that approached the election of 1964. Woodrow Lloyd, who had taken over as premier, didn't enjoy the same popularity as Douglas, and feelings were still raw for many over the Medicare fight. The Liberals under Ross Thatcher scored a narrow victory. Thatcher's government immediately set itself up as a champion of private enterprise, cutting the budget, raising Medicare fees, and beginning to sell off Crown corporations and other assets. Thatcher offered financial rewards to companies investing in Saskatchewan potash and pulp mills, and began an attack against unions and centralized power.

The prosperity of the fifties continued and a boom in the mid-sixties briefly made Saskatoon the country's fastest growing city. For the first time since federal equalization payments had begun in the thirties, Saskatchewan was moved from "have not" to "have"

Turbine on the Gardiner Dam, on the South Saskatchewan River. The dam was completed in 1967, Canada's Centennial year. In a rare show of non-partisanship, it was named after James Gardiner, a former Liberal premier who went on to be federal agriculture minister; the lake it created was named for Conservative John Diefenbaker; and a park beside it was named for Tommy Douglas.

status, and phasing out of payments began. An economic downturn toward the end of the decade, along with a wheat glut and lower prices, tarnished the government's image of private enterprise. There was controversy over Liberal plans for a new pulp mill in the north, and there were divisions within the party itself over pollution concerns and the government's anti-labour stand. The election of June 1971 saw a revitalized NDP, under Allan Blakeney, win a decisive victory. Thatcher died a month later, at 54. He had been a strong leader and left the Liberals disorganized and demoralized.

Blakeney and Devine

The NDP under Blakeney reversed several trends established by Thatcher. Government involvement again increased. SaskOil was created as a way of tapping petroleum riches for the government, and a number of mines were purchased to create the Potash Corporation of Saskatchewan. On the social front, the government cancelled Medicare premiums and began free dental care for children and a subsidized prescription drug plan. Community colleges were set up, and the Saskatchewan Indian Federated College was established as part of the University of Regina, which became a separate institution.

Saskatchewan was fairly prosperous through the seventies. Agriculture, which had once totally dominated the economy, was playing a smaller and smaller role. The Liberals held on as the Opposition through the 1975 election, but they were wiped out in 1978. The Conservatives emerged as the Opposition, paving the way for Grant Devine's landslide win in 1982. Like Thatcher before him, Devine proclaimed himself and his government the champions of private enterprise and set about dismantling many of the NDP's programs. The Conservatives won the 1986 election with a reduced majority, and their popularity waned even further towards the end of the decade as the province — and the country — sank into recession. In late 1991, the NDP, with Roy Romanow at the helm, swept them out of office.

Romanow's chief goal was to turn around the runaway deficit spending that, under a decade of Conservative rule, had built up a $15 billion debt. Belts were tightened throughout the public sector and before the end of his first term, the deficit, over $1 billion a year when he was elected, had been eliminated. Despite widespread unhappiness over their policies, Romanow and the NDP government was decisively re-elected in 1995. The Liberals, under their first woman leader, Lynda Haverstock, emerged as the official opposition. Despite her success, though, the party turned on Haverstock and she was replaced as leader by newcomer Ron Osika.

Looking Ahead

As Saskatchewan entered the nineties, its people were becoming increasingly conscious of environmental issues. Concern over pollution first arose during the seventies, with outcries over chemical spills, mercury in lakes, and the effects of development in the north. A Round Table on the Environment, sponsored by the government, examined a wide range of matters relating to preservation of land, water and air quality. A nuclear reactor deal with Atomic Energy of Canada was cancelled.

As economic conditions changed during the eighties, poverty became

Smoke from the Aspenite Mill at the town of Hudson Bay

an issue for the first time since the end of the Depression. By 1991, there were 11 food banks operating in the province, the poverty rate was the highest in the country, and the new NDP government, with a large debt to worry about, was hard put to find ways to alleviate the situation. Child poverty, which the NDP had vowed to eliminate, had actually gotten worse by the time of the 1995 election.

But Saskatchewan remains Next Year Country. The Saskatchewan character and outlook were shaped by people's relationship to the land, the harsh conditions of pioneer life, the nightmare of the thirties. Out of this developed a distrust of institutions, an interest in local government as a tool, and a passion for political action. Whether as Natives overwhelmed by a foreign culture, as immigrants facing enormous adjustment problems or as farmers at the mercy of nature's whims, Saskatchewanians have learned the importance of both self-reliance and co-operation. More than any other Canadians, perhaps, they cherish their traditions of working and living together. And they take great pride in their ability not just to survive adversity but to overcome it.

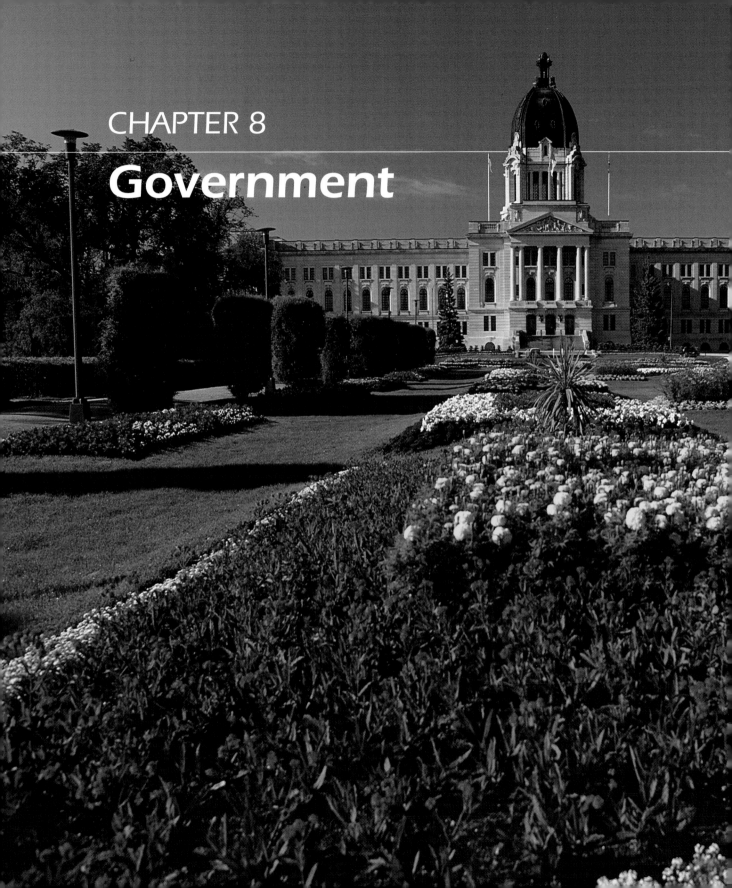

CHAPTER 8

Government

Saskatchewan entered Confederation on September 1, 1905. It is thus a very young political jurisdiction, even though its history as a place of human habitation is long.

Like all provinces, Saskatchewan is governed in the British parliamentary tradition, with a Lieutenant-Governor, who represents the Crown, and a government made up of a premier, cabinet and legislative assembly. The premier and the cabinet operate as an executive council, which actually runs the government, while the legislature enacts laws.

The government is more than a handful of politicians, however. Cabinet members are the heads of departments, but beneath them is a large bureaucracy staffed by some 25 000 civil servants who look after everything from education and health to highways, forests, oil wells, tourism and, of course, taxes.

Federal

When Saskatchewan became a province, it was granted all of the powers of other provinces with two key exceptions: control over land and natural resources. The federal government finally gave up these powers in 1930, but it still holds sole jurisdiction in areas such as banking and national defence. The two governments share jurisdiction in several other areas, including health, education and culture.

Saskatchewan elects 14 members to the federal Parliament and has six appointed representatives in the Senate.

There are about 10 000 federal employees in the province.

Legislative Building, Regina

Local

Saskatchewan people are famous for their passionate approach to politics. They seem to also have a passion for government. Just look at how much local government they have: 12 cities, 144 towns, 325 villages, 39 resort villages, 2 northern towns, 13 northern villages, 12 northern hamlets, 298 rural municipalities and 141 organized hamlets. Of these 986 municipalities, 701 have a population of less than 1000, and 117 have less than 100. Saskatchewan has more municipalities than Alberta and Manitoba combined and almost matches the number in Ontario, which has ten times the population.

These local governments look after streets, sewers, garbage pickup, police and fire-fighting and a long list of other local concerns. Together, they have over 12 000 employees.

Regina, Saskatoon and a few other communities have their own police forces. Policing of the rest of Saskatchewan is handled by the Royal Canadian Mounted Police on a contract with the federal government. The RCMP presence in the province is enhanced by its academy, located in Regina. All RCMP recruits spend six months training there.

The Justice System

There are three levels of provincial courts. The lowest, called the Provincial Court, deals with minor criminal offences and the early stages of major ones. An upper court, the Court of Queen's Bench, deals with cases involving serious crimes and civil suits. The Saskatchewan Court of Appeal is the province's highest court. It deals with appeals from both lower courts, and its decisions can be appealed to the Supreme Court of Canada. Provincial Court judges and the justices of the Court of Queen's Bench and the Appeal Court are appointed by the federal government on the advice of the provincial Minister of Justice.

The Sergeant-major's noon parade at the RCMP training centre in Regina

Government Finance

Saskatchewan levies a wide range of provincial taxes and fees, including personal income tax, corporate income tax and sales tax. The sales tax is 9 percent, with a few categories of goods (such as food, clothing, books, drugs) exempt. There are also taxes on gasoline and other fuels, taxes and royalties on mining and petroleum extraction, as well as motor vehicle licences and fees, and other smaller ones. All these taxes raise a lot of money for the provincial government but not enough to cover all its expenses. Saskatchewan also gets about 25 percent of its budget from the federal government. This money is earmarked for health, education, welfare and other purposes. Because Ottawa has changed its revenue-sharing formulas, however, this amount is declining, causing serious economic upheaval. Local governments rely primarily on property taxes, business taxes, and utility charges and a variety of other usage fees. They also get provincial and, to a lesser extent, federal transfers and grants.

Education

Schools came to Saskatchewan with the missionaries. The earliest one was probably the one established at Cumberland House in 1840 by Henry Budd, a Cree who was trained at a Church of England school in Red River. The first public school was opened in 1878 in Battleford, paid for by donations; opening of the first publicly funded school followed two years later.

Above: Elementary school students and their teachers enjoy a visit from the Saskatoon Symphony Orchestra.
Right: Elder Bette Spence counsels a student and her child at the Saskatchewan Indian Federated College. Elders are an integral part of the college and are often sought out for personal advice.

The North-West Territories Act of 1875 granted the right for education in the Territories and for a system of minority separate schools (for either Protestants or Catholics). As it happened, however, control of schools continued to be an issue.

The act of Parliament that created the province of Saskatchewan guaranteed some minority education rights. But over the years, there has had to be a struggle to preserve Catholic schools and French language education. The use of French in schools was banned for a time, but it was later restored, and in the early 1990s francophones won a long battle for the right to establish their own separate school boards.

In the 1994-95 school year, over 275 000 students were enrolled in the province's 872 public and separate schools, nine regional colleges, two universities and one technical institute. They are taught by some 16 000 teachers, instructors and professors. The universities awarded 4364 degrees in 1991. That number is declining, however, as tuitions soar.

The emphasis Saskatchewan residents have always put on education has paid off. The province has the highest high school graduation rate in the country — 75 percent — and the highest literacy rate, with over 70 percent of the population in the highest level of reading ability.

Health

Even more than education, Saskatchewan has placed great value on health. It was the first province to have a hospitalization plan for all residents and pioneered Medicare. In 1991, Saskatchewan had more acute-care hospitals (134) than any province but Ontario and led the nation in the ratio of hospital beds per resident (6.8 per 1000). The NDP government, however, has launched a massive reform of health care services, converting over 50 acute-care hospitals into "health centres" and drastically lowering the bed-per-patient ratio.

CHAPTER 9
The Economy

When the Progressive Conservatives took office in Saskatchewan in 1982, Premier Grant Devine made a boast he would later regret: the province's economy was so robust it could be mismanaged and still break even.

In the previous decade, world prices had been high for a number of goods that Saskatchewan has in abundance: wheat, oil, potash, uranium, goods that are the bedrock of the province's economy. No sooner had Devine spoken than — through no fault of his — the situation changed drastically. World prices plummeted for those goods. At the same time, high interest rates, which were battering all of Canada, took a particularly heavy toll on Saskatchewan farmers, who must constantly borrow. To make matters worse, several years of drought had a devastating effect on crops. As a result, farmers by the thousands lost their land, and people left the province in droves during the latter half of the eighties.

One bright spot has been the unemployment rate, consistently the lowest in the country. Others are the inflation rate, second lowest in the country in 1995, and the low price of real estate. Saskatchewan is just about the cheapest province in which to live, even though its taxes are the nation's highest and its median income — $15 700 in 1993 — is third lowest. The province's outlook is derived from its large farm population, which is used to having crops — and dreams — wiped out by too little rain, or too much rain, early frost and low prices. "Maybe next year," the farmer says, wiping his brow. Saskatchewan is Next Year Country.

Canola fields in bloom. In recent years, canola has become Saskatchewan's third most valuable crop.

Diversification

"Hewers of wood, haulers of water."

That curious phrase is often used to describe people and regions thought of as doing little more than manual labour: cutting wood, carrying buckets of water. In Saskatchewan, a variation on it might be "harvesters of wheat." The province grows more of that grain than the rest of the country put together, and during the first three decades of its existence, wheat wasn't just the backbone of the economy, it *was* the economy. A decade of depression and drought taught Saskatchewan a bitter lesson about the perils of putting all its eggs in one basket. In the years since the Second World War, the agriculture of the province has been diversified, and Saskatchewan farmers now grow a wide range of grains and other crops. Provincial governments have also laboured mightily — with considerable success — to further expand the economy by backing mining development, petroleum exploration and manufacturing sectors. Still, the province remains largely a supplier of raw materials.

Agriculture

Saskatchewan, with just a tiny fraction of Canada's land, contains a third of the nation's farms and almost half of its cultivated land.

Agriculture produces only about a tenth of the economic wealth of the province, but its impact is far greater than that figure suggests. One in five jobs — 80 000 — are in agriculture, and another 40 000 are indirectly dependent on it.

Flying into Regina or driving across Saskatchewan on the Trans-Canada Highway, it would be easy to conclude that the province is nothing but a giant wheat field. Of course, it isn't, but Saskatchewan does have over 15 million hectares (37 million acres) of farmland in production with more than half in wheat. Out of those fields came pouring over 24 million tonnes of crops in 1994, including, along with the wheat, oats, barley, canola, sunflowers, lentils, even canary

Above: Spraying crops at Denholm.
Left: Harvesting. In 1996,
Saskatchewan had almost 8 million
hectares (19 million acres) planted in
wheat.

seed. Saskatchewan farmers also produce large amounts of cattle,
hogs, chicken, turkey, eggs, milk, honey and a variety of vegetables.

Saskatchewan is the third biggest agricultural earner, behind
Quebec and Ontario. And wheat remains the single most important
crop, with some 90 percent destined for export. But grain prices do
a good yo-yo imitation. In 1980, wheat was about $300 a tonne; in
the summer of 1991, it was around the $75 mark, but by 1996 had
rebounded to around $200. Expenses, on the other hand, steadily
rise — Saskatchewan farmers spend about $4 billion a year on seed,
fertilizer, livestock, fuel, machinery, land and interest on their loans.
As a result, the average farmer was left with just $9000 take-home
pay in 1991 — but strikingly down from 1986, the last really good
year for farmers.

Things have improved markedly since then, with average
incomes rising to almost $16 000 in 1993 (augmented by another
$30 000 in off-farm income). Saskatchewan farmers registered their
highest sales ever in 1994, recording more than $5 billion in total
cash receipts. As a result, farm debt has declined noticeably.

Roundup time in Denholm. *Inset:* **Harvesting potatoes in the Qu'Appelle Valley, north of Regina**

The economics of farming have been changing dramatically, with fewer farms (60 000) but bigger farms — an average of just over 400 hectares (about 1000 acres). Low prices and high debt have made Saskatchewan farmers dependent on government aid. Federal farm programs include marketing boards, hail insurance, the Farm Credit Corporation and the Farm Debt Review Assistance Program.

Mines and Minerals

Saskatchewan's second richest harvest also comes from the ground. Beneath the soil are rich deposits of minerals and petroleum, worth almost $4 billion a year.

One of Saskatchewan's earliest exports was buffalo bones — thousands of tonnes of them, shipped by rail to Chicago, where they

Potash mine at Allan. Most of the province's potash deposits lie in the area just south of Saskatoon and in the southeast, near the Manitoba border.

were ground into fertilizer. Now the province is the world's largest exporter of another commodity used for fertilizer — potash. In fact, Saskatchewan has over half of the world's recoverable potash reserves, so it will be a valuable resource for many years to come. A quarter of the world's supply was produced by 2700 workers at Saskatchewan's 10 mines in 1995, and was worth almost $1.1 billion.

Saskatchewan and Ontario are Canada's only producers of uranium, and Saskatchewan's three mines produce enough to make it the world's largest exporter, with about a fourth of the world market. In 1995, Saskatchewan's 1000 uranium miners dug 5000 tonnes of the radioactive metal, worth over $400 million.

Gold mining has been becoming increasingly important in recent years, but silver mining is declining. Saskatchewan also produces small amounts of copper, zinc, salt, sand, gravel and clay.

Energy

Although overshadowed by Alberta in output of both oil and gas, the province is still a major producer. In 1995, its wells pumped up over $2.3 billion worth of the stuff that makes the machine age move and hum. Even with the business in a slump due to low world prices, some 8000 Saskatchewan jobs are dependent on it. Drilling of new wells has revived following the recession of the early '90s, and the province earned a record $200 million from the sale of mineral rights in 1994.

Oil well in western Saskatchewan. *Inset:* Heavy oil upgrader at Lloydminster

Saskatchewan has two conventional refineries and Canada's first heavy oil upgrader, a sophisticated plant, located in Regina, that processes previously unusable heavy oil at a rate of 50 000 barrels a day. A second such plant was built in the early nineties at Lloydminster on the Saskatchewan-Alberta border. The province has the world's largest reserve of heavy oil, a thick, sludgy mixture of oil and sand. Unfortunately, it's very expensive to recover and refine.

Saskatchewan produces no bituminous coal but has Canada's only supply of lignite — less valuable because it burns quickly and gives off less heat, but cleaner burning. Miners dug up around 9 million tonnes in 1995, worth about $100 million. Almost all of it goes to SaskPower, the province's electrical utility, for power generation. Small amounts go to Ontario and Manitoba for the same purpose.

Manufacturing and Trade

Trade is essential to Saskatchewan's economy, with one in four of all jobs trade-related. About half of the province's products are exported.

The province had around 1400 manufacturers in 1995, almost double the number a decade earlier. Most of them are small, though there were nine manufacturers with sales of over $50 million. As might be expected, food products are the major focus, with annual sales of over $1 billion, but Saskatchewan also produces a wide range of goods, from steel to fertilizer, street sweepers to ambulances, diapers to enamel pins. One of the biggest manufacturers is Ipsco, the Regina steelmaker, with sales of over $500 million. There are over 26 000 people employed in the manufacturing sector, led by food processing and followed by printing, machinery, fabricated metal products, wood and electrical and electronics industries.

Forests, Fish and Furs

While a large part of northern Saskatchewan is forested, harvesting of timber plays a relatively small part in the province's economy. In 1995, over 3300 Saskatchewan loggers and pulp mill workers cut down and processed close to $335 million worth of wood and wood products.

The idea of a fishery in land-locked Saskatchewan may seem laughable, but the province's many lakes do produce a certain amount of commercially caught whitefish, walleye, pike and other fish. About 2000 commercial fishermen harvest more than 2.5 million kilograms (5.5 million pounds) of fish annually. Most of the catch is sold to the U.S. and Europe.

Trapping, once the mainstay of economic activity in the area, continues to put money in the pockets of some 4500 trappers, but less and less each year. This is due in large part to the efforts of the worldwide animal rights movement to change people's attitudes toward fur. Trapping brings in less than $1 million, down from a sum five times larger just a few years ago.

Harvested logs arrive at the mill in Hudson Bay.

Transport

When the CCF came to power in 1944, it began a program of road building that over the years has given Saskatchewan more roadway than any other province. Adding in municipal streets and alleys, there's about 250 000 kilometres (155 000 miles) worth, of which about one-tenth is provincial highway. The province also has 940 bridges and operates 13 free ferries across the Saskatchewan River and its two branches.

All that highway costs money: in 1995, over $300 million was spent on building and repairing highways, roads, streets and bridges by all levels of government. And, of course, those roads get used: there are over 750 000 cars, trucks, buses and motorcycles in the province. Between them, they burn up over a billion litres (260 million gallons) of gasoline.

Saskatchewan has a long and proud railway history, and there are still over 4000 kilometres (2500 miles) of mainline track in the province, though passenger rail service is just a fond memory now in Regina and other southern Saskatchewan cities. VIA Rail shut down its southern route in 1989, but its northern route still runs through Saskatoon.

The province has two major airports, in Regina and Saskatoon, and 180 or so smaller airports and landing strips.

Lakes teeming with fish attract many tourists to Saskatchewan.

Tourism

Tourism has become increasingly important to Saskatchewan, worth an estimated $900 million in 1996 and growing at about 4 percent a year. There are an estimated 8 million "trips" by individuals in the province annually, with the majority of them by Saskatchewan residents themselves. The government has been focusing its tourism advertising on increasing the 6 percent share represented by foreigners, mainly Americans.

Communications

Saskatchewan has four daily newspapers: the Regina *Leader-Post*, the Saskatoon *Star-Phoenix*, the Moose Jaw *Times-Herald* and the Prince Albert *Daily Herald*. In addition, there are around 80 weekly newspapers. Radio came to the province in 1922; there are now 18 AM radio stations and 10 FM stations, including Radio-Canada (French CBC) service. The province also has 39 television stations, again including Radio-Canada.

The province's Crown-owned telephone company, SaskTel, is the fourth largest system in Canada, with revenues of close to $600 million and about 4000 employees.

CHAPTER 10
Arts and Recreation

Saskatchewan people work hard, and they like to play hard. A cornucopia of cultural opportunities have developed in the province, along with sports and recreational activities of all types.

The arts were given a big boost with the creation of the Saskatchewan Arts Board in 1948. The first organization of its kind in North America, it was modelled on the British Arts Council. In its early years, it supported drama and music tours, and was behind the establishment of a summer school of the arts — the much loved Fort San — at a former tuberculosis sanatorium near Fort Qu'Appelle. For years, hundreds of young musicians, dancers and artists trained there, and prominent literary figures like W.O. Mitchell, Rudy Wiebe and Eli Mandel led writing workshops. Today, the Arts Board gives individual grants to writers, filmmakers, musicians, dancers and artists, and provides operating funds to galleries, orchestras, theatres and publishers.

The Arts Board also helped the Organization of Saskatchewan Arts Councils get started in the mid-1960s. OSAC is the booking agent for Saskatchewan's 69 arts councils, bringing talent to Saskatchewan that individual towns could never afford on their own. OSAC also sponsors travelling art shows and a wide variety of workshops.

Cultural, recreational and educational organizations received a badly needed financial shot in the arm in 1974 when the government designated sports, recreation and culture as beneficiaries of profits generated by the new lotteries craze. Thousands of activities have been made possible as a result of Saskatchewanians' love of small-scale gambling. And hundreds of thousands of people benefit in

Corretta and *Anita*, **bronze sculptures by Saskatchewan artist Joe Fafard**

Ukrainian dancers dazzle their audience at one of Saskatchewan's many multicultural celebrations.

some way: as individual artists or athletes who receive grants or awards; as members of cultural, sports or recreation groups whose activities have expanded; as students taking classes in heritage languages, bird-watching or ethnic cooking; or as audiences at concerts, poetry readings, track meets or curling bonspiels.

Writing and Theatre

Two of the finest novels ever published in Canada were written by Saskatchewan writers: *As For Me and My House* by Sinclair Ross and *Who Has Seen the Wind* by W.O. Mitchell. Since those landmark books appeared in the 1940s, Saskatchewan has often been in the forefront of the Canadian literary world.

Through the fifties and sixties, novelists like Edward McCourt, who set many of his books in a vividly described prairie landscape, and poets like Eli Mandel, whose verse often recalls the Saskatchewan of Depression times, continued the literary tradition. Recently, many writers have reversed the trend set by Ross, Mitchell and Mandel, who felt they had to leave the province to achieve

Left: The Shakespeare on the Saskatchewan Festival is famous for placing Shakespeare in innovative settings. Seen here, the 1991 production of *As You Like It. Above:* The Saskatoon Native Theatre grew out of the drama program at Joe Duquette High School. The plays presented are written collectively and performed by the students.

success. Guy Vanderhaeghe, winner of a 1982 Governor General's Award for his short story collection *Man Descending,* lives in Saskatoon; Sharon Butala, whose novels and odes to country living are bestsellers, lives on a ranch in Cypress Hills. Ken Mitchell has continued a prolific outpouring of novels, plays and poetry while teaching at the University of Regina.

Connie Gault, Dianne Warren and a new generation of playwrights are starting to put Saskatchewan on the country's dramatic map as well. Saskatoon has emerged as a theatre capital, with four to choose from plus the Shakespeare on the Saskatchewan riverside summer theatre and an annual "fringe" festival in the summer. In Regina, theatre-goers have fewer choices, but their first is the Globe Theatre, the oldest professional theatre in the province, started by Ken and Sue Kramer in 1966. The Globe's mainstage season offers over 100 performances at its 400-seat theatre-in-the-round.

Amateur theatrics are also popular, the Saskatchewan Drama League having formed in 1933 to hold contests and festivals. There are 75 amateur theatre groups in the province, the overwhelming majority of them in rural areas.

Film lovers from around Canada are drawn to Saskatchewan every spring where the Yorkton Short Film and Video Festival showcases up to 350 entries. Begun in 1950, it is the oldest continually running film festival in North America.

Visual Arts

Saskatchewan has a rich tradition of visual arts dating back to prehistoric Native artists. The province's first professional painters came west early in the century. They were encouraged by Regina art collector Norman MacKenzie, whose name graces the city's new $10 million public art gallery, which opened in 1990.

Augustus Kenderdine joined the University of Saskatchewan as an art lecturer in 1927. Later, he moved to Regina College, establishing a school of art in 1936 with funds bequeathed by MacKenzie. The Emma Lake Summer School of Art opened the same year. Later, under the leadership of Kenneth Lochhead, the Regina art school became one of the best in the country.

Fred S. Mendel, a meat-packing magnate, was to Saskatoon what

Below: **Landscape by Dorothy Knowles entitled** *Et In Arcadia Ego. Right:* **The Mendel Art Gallery in Saskatoon**

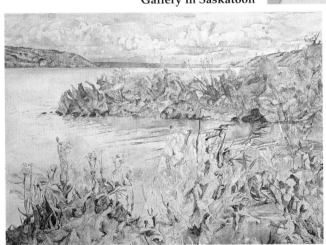

Norman MacKenzie was to Regina, leaving his art collection and money for a gallery to the city. Today, the Mendel Art Gallery enjoys a better attendance rate than any other gallery in Canada except the National in Ottawa.

The original Norman MacKenzie Art Gallery opened in 1953. Among well-known artists working in Saskatchewan then were Lochhead, Ted Godwin, Ron Bloore, Dorothy Knowles, William Perehudoff and Illingworth Kerr. Artists prominent in the sixties and to the present include R.D. Symons, David Thauberger, and Allen Sapp, a Cree painter from North Battleford who has received international attention. Jack Sures and Vic Cicansky were at the forefront of a ceramics boom in Regina, and sculptor Joe Fafard's human and animal figures have earned him an international reputation.

Music

Music has been stirring the hearts of Saskatchewanians since a small orchestra conducted by British immigrant Frank Laubach played his composition "The Saskatchewan March and Two-Step" at ceremonies celebrating the province's entry into Confederation. The Regina Philharmonic Orchestra, with Laubach as its conductor, actually preceded provincehood; formed in 1904, it is the oldest continually

The Regina Symphony Orchestra

Top Left: **Buffy Sainte-Marie at the Regina Folk Festival.** *Top Right:* **In the early nineties, The Northern Pikes, Saskatchewanians all, become one of the country's top rock groups.** *Right:* **Hart Rouge. The** *fransaskois* **sisters and brother have put the name of Willow Bunch, their hometown, on the international pop music map.**

operating symphony orchestra in the country. Saskatoon has a symphony orchestra as well, and both cities have dance troupes and opera guilds.

Laubach also organized the Saskatchewan Music Festival Association in 1908. Today, the music festival is as much a spring tradition in many communities as the first robin. Some 75 000 Saskatchewan youngsters take part in dozens of well-attended music and dance festivals held throughout the province.

The province is home to a wide variety of other music festivals, including the Saskatoon Jazz Festival and the annual Regina Folk Festival — the only free folk festival in the country. Probably the best known musical event is the Big Valley Jamboree, held at Craven, in the Qu'Appelle Valley, every July. This country music extravaganza draws as many as 30 000 country music lovers from around the country and the United States.

Among Saskatchewan-born musicians who have made it on the larger stage are opera stars Jon Vickers from Prince Albert and Irene Salemka of Weyburn; singer-songwriter Joni Mitchell from Saskatoon; singer-songwriter Buffy Sainte-Marie, born on the Piapot Reserve north of Regina; blues singer-guitarist Colin James from Regina; and several very successful rock groups, including the Northern Pikes, the Waltons and the francophone Hart Rouge.

Museums

Saskatchewan has about 300 public museums of all types — more museums per capita than any other province. They range from the Royal Saskatchewan Museum, the province's pride and joy, to dozens of small, volunteer-run museums, often in converted school houses or railway stations, in villages and towns across the province. Falling in between, to mention just a few, are the RCMP Museum and the Saskatchewan Sports Hall of Fame in Regina and the Western Development Museums in Saskatoon, Moose Jaw, Yorkton and North Battleford. In 1992, the new Wanuskewin Heritage Park, just north of Saskatoon, opened with Native artifacts dating back 8000 years.

Recreation

Saskatchewan boasts some of the best fishing and hunting in North America. Over 100 000 lakes, reservoirs, streams and rivers are home to 68 species of fish and attract hordes of tourists. Sportsfishing is estimated to generate more than $200 million in annual economic activity in the province. As for hunters, thousands of them take to the fields and woods in pursuit of deer, elk, moose, bear, upland game birds and waterfowl.

Saskatchewanians also love camping, hiking, canoeing and skiing, and seize every opportunity to enjoy the province's millions of

In summer, Saskatchewanians take enthusiastically to the province's lakes and streams.

hectares of public parkland. There are close to 4 million visits yearly to the 31 provincial parks, 212 protected areas, 8 historic sites, 152 recreation sites and a hundred-odd regional parks. There were thousands of other visits to Prince Albert National Park and to Grasslands National Park, still in the formative stage in southwest Saskatchewan grazing country.

Sports

Few things gladden the hearts of Saskatchewan people as much as the Roughriders, the professional football team located in Regina but belonging to the entire province. The often also-ran Roughriders seem to capture the spirit of the Saskatchewan farming community, which is always dreaming about better luck next year. And, just as farmers sometimes have bumper years, the Roughriders sometimes have winning seasons — in fact, they dominated western football in the twenties and thirties, playing in (but losing) seven Grey Cup games. Again from the mid-sixties to the mid-seventies, the team, led by quarterback Ron Lancaster and running back George Reed, played in five league championships, winning in 1966. More recently,

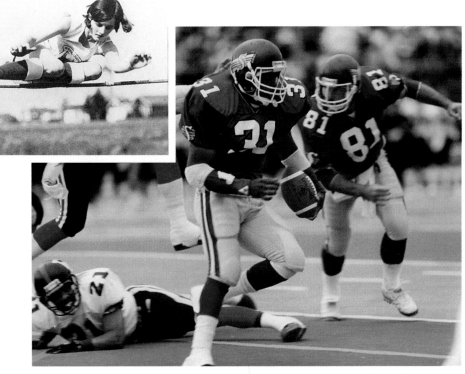

The Saskatchewan Roughriders (in green) in action against the Ottawa Rough Riders. *Inset:* High jumper Ethel Catherwood, nicknamed The Saskatoon Lily, won the gold medal in the 1928 Olympics.

they experienced a Cinderella season in 1989 when they beat the Hamilton Tiger-Cats in one of the most thrilling Grey Cup games ever.

On weekends when the Riders aren't doing combat at Taylor Field, the junior Regina Rams often are, sometimes against their arch-rivals, the Saskatoon Hilltops. And when football season ends, the ice is already crackling under the skates of junior hockey stars of the Western Hockey League's five Saskatchewan teams from Regina, Saskatoon, Prince Albert, Moose Jaw and Swift Current, and those of Saskatchewan Junior Hockey League teams.

The sports scene has been enlivened in the past couple of years by the appearance of the Regina Cyclone and Saskatoon Riot, teams in the professional Northern Baseball League. And in the ever-popular sport of curling, the Sandra Peterson rink brought international honours to Saskatchewan by winning the Women's World Championship in 1993 and '94, adding to the four championships earned by the Ernie Richardson rink in the early '60s. Saskatchewan curling teams skipped by Rick Folk and Marge Mitchell won world championships in 1980 as well.

CHAPTER 11

Around the Province

This page, top: The Snowbirds, Canada's famous aerobatics team, are based at CFB Moose Jaw; *middle:* The rolling ranchland of the Vermillion Hills, west of Moose Jaw; *bottom:* farm life near Warman. *Opposite page, top:* Fort Battleford in winter; *middle:* Viking ship sailing on Wascana Lake as part of Regina's Mosaic festival; *bottom:* grain elevator and train at Delmas; *inset:* "nodding donkey" pumping oil at Lloydminster

Anyone who thinks Saskatchewan is flat and boring should take a look at the sparkling waters of the Clearwater River and the lush spruce and aspen forest through which it winds. Or watch the morning sun struggle to pierce through the purplish mist that clings to the shore where the North Saskatchewan and Battle rivers meet at historic Battleford. Or stand at a lookout atop the Cypress Hills to see all of the southwestern portion of the province laid out like a richly woven carpet of browns, greens and blues.

Rival Cities

Separated by about 260 kilometres (160 miles) and virtually identical in size, Regina and Saskatoon are — not surprisingly — perennial rivals. Despite their similarity in size and age, the cities are very different in character. Regina is a government town, its economy made stable by thousands of civil servants and workers at bank, insurance and co-op head offices. Saskatoon is more of a university town, with a more adventurous and varied intellectual and cultural life.

Regina

Regina (named for Queen Victoria) suffers from an undeserved poor reputation that bewilders the 180 000 Reginans. They love their city for its relatively slow pace, its compact size and the good manners and friendliness of its inhabitants. Writer Pierre Berton once described Regina as the city that had done the most with the least, and it's true that Regina didn't start with much. Built on a flat, treeless plain of dense gumbo that turns to Crazy Glue in the rain, the city is endlessly

battered by wind. It is, moreover, one of the few — if not the only —
major North American city not built on a lake or river — though its
famous Wascana Creek, originally known as Pile of Bones, is the
remnant of what was once a massive glacial lake.

Over the years, however, Reginans have created a lake and more
park space than any other city in the country but Ottawa; they have
planted over 200 000 trees along Regina's wide, clean streets, and put
up some interesting structures, like the S-curved SaskPower Building
on Victoria Avenue and the twin diagonally sliced buildings
guarding the entrance to the Scarth Street Mall.

Regina's pride and joy is Wascana Centre, a government reserve in
the heart of the city whose 930 hectares (2300 acres) make it the

Regina scenes, *clockwise
from far left:* a literally
hair-raising experience at
the Saskatchewan Science
Centre; downtown street;
Canada geese on Wascana
Lake

largest urban park in North America. The Centre's focal point is Wascana Lake, created in 1908 by damming Wascana Creek. The Legislative Building, the University of Regina, a couple of hospitals, the MacKenzie Art Gallery, the Centre of the Arts and a handful of other government buildings can all be found within the rambling grounds of the park. Wascana Centre is also home to the restored cabin in which John Diefenbaker spent part of his boyhood.

Wascana Lake ends abruptly at Albert Street, Regina's main thoroughfare. On the other side of the dam trickles tiny Wascana Creek. As a result, the Albert Memorial Bridge has been dubbed "the longest bridge over the shortest body of water in the world." Bicyclers, walkers and, in winter, cross-country skiers like to head west from here along the Devonian Pathway, a ten-kilometre (six-mile) trail that follows the creek as it winds its way through the city.

Not far off is the largest exhibition complex west of Toronto, home of the Buffalo Days fair held every summer, and of Agribition, a farm show and rodeo held every fall. Queensbury Downs racetrack is a year-round attraction at the exhibition ground. Just east of it is the Sportsplex fieldhouse and a couple of blocks further on, Taylor Field, home of the Roughriders.

Further west is Government House, once the home of Lieutenant-Governors, now restored to its turn-of-the-century grandeur and open to the public. Nearby, the RCMP Academy, with its museum, chapel and colourful Sunset Retreat Ceremony, is a magnet to history buffs. Other attractions include the Royal Saskatchewan Museum and the Saskatchewan Sports Hall of Fame, both in the downtown area, and the Regina Plains Museum, located along with the Globe Theatre in the renovated Old City Hall.

In Victoria Park, just across one street from the public library and across another from the stately old Hotel Saskatchewan, which recently received a $20-million renovation, is a plaque commemorating the 1885 trial and execution of Louis Riel. A play based on the transcript of the trial has been performed in the city every summer since 1966. Victoria Park is home to the annual Regina Folk Festival.

Saskatoon

Saskatoon began its modern life in 1883 as a settlement of the Temperance Colonization Society, a Methodist group from Ontario looking for a refuge from the evils of hard drink. A noble experiment, but it didn't last long. Today, Saskatoon, which takes its name from the delicious wild berries that still grow in profusion in the area, is a modern, sophisticated city of almost 190 000 people.

Seven bridges span the South Saskatchewan River, which divides the city, giving it its nickname of Bridge City. The central area, anchored by the stately Bessborough Hotel, Anglican and Roman Catholic cathedrals and the Mendel Art Gallery, is on the west bank. On the higher east bank is the sprawling campus of the University of Saskatchewan, the Broadway area, with its book stores and cafés catering to a large student crowd, and the Nutana neighbourhood, a remnant of the old temperance colony. The John G. Diefenbaker Centre, a museum dedicated to the province's most famous son, is

Below left: It's easy to see why Saskatoon has been nicknamed The City of Bridges. *Below right:* One of Saskatoon's many parks. *Inset:* The stately Bessborough Hotel remains one of Saskatoon's most imposing buildings.

on the campus, and the former prime minister's grave is nearby, on the brow of a hill overlooking the river. All of the river bank is parkland and 15 kilometres (9 miles) of trail follows it through the city. On Summer weekends, the trail is crowded with bikers and strollers enjoying the sunshine and watching the pelicans feeding.

Saskatoon is home to several other sites of particular interest, including the Western Development Museum, which documents pioneer life in the province, and two Ukrainian museums. The demonstration farm at the university and the Forestry Farm with its zoo also attract many visitors.

Rural Saskatchewan

Because Saskatchewan was so recently settled, much of its history is close to the surface and readily available to anyone willing to seek it out. So too is its beauty — the subtle beauty of the prairies and the more dramatic beauty of the province's many less-known treasures.

The tourist industry has divided the province into five zones. Let's look at them one at a time.

Cowboy Country

The southwest, cowboy and dinosaur country, is dominated by the densely forested Cypress Hills, one of the two areas in the province high enough to have escaped being totally covered during the last Ice Age. Vegetation and fossils found nowhere else in the province are mute evidence of an earlier age destroyed by the glaciers.

The recent discovery of the almost complete skeleton of a Tyrannosaurus Rex in the Frenchman River valley below the hills has turned the small ranching town of Eastend, where the bones are housed in a temporary museum, into a bustling tourist destination. The giant dinosaur, dubbed Scotty, is the star of a 1996 large-screen Imax movie.

Legends of the Old West seem to come alive at rebuilt Fort Walsh, the first North-West Mounted Police post in the territory, and Farwell's Post, site of the Cypress Hills Massacre in 1873. North of the Trans-Canada Highway are the rolling dunes of the Great Sand Hills, as dry and barren as the Sahara, and Lake Diefenbaker, a boating and water-skiing paradise. South of the highway, which leads from Maple Creek to Swift Current to Moose Jaw, are Grasslands National Park and the adobe hills of Wood Mountain, where Sitting Bull and 5000 Lakota Sioux sought refuge after the Battle of Little Bighorn. The Wood Mountain Stampede is the oldest continually running rodeo in Canada.

Further east is St. Victor, a sacred place where centuries-old petroglyphs depicting Native life can be seen. At the southeastern corner of the zone are the starkly dramatic Big Muddy Badlands, a wild moonscape of deep ravines and eroded sandstone. Caves in these badlands were used as hideouts by legendary American outlaws like the gang known as the Wild Bunch.

The Southeast

Zone 2, the classic prairie of the southeast, takes in the breathtaking beauty of the Qu'Appelle Valley north of Regina and the arid coal and

Left: **Fort Walsh, a reconstruction of the early North-West Mounted Police post.** *Below:* **At the northern edge of the Big Muddy Badlands, fortress-like Castle Butte rises 60 m. (200 ft.) above the prairie.** *Inset:* **Moose Jaw is Saskatchewan's third-largest city.**

Above: Visitors get a glimpse of how a prosperous farm family lived around 1912 at Motherwell Homestead National Historic Park. *Right:* Roche Percée. Eroded by wind and water, this extraordinary rock formation is covered with petroglyphs carved by generations of Indians.

gas country of the south near the small cities of Weyburn and Estevan. The latter, with an average 2540 sunny hours a year, is Canada's sunshine capital. Nearby are fields of nodding oil donkeys, massive open-pit coal mines and the small French town of Bienfait, pronounced locally "bean fate."

The Qu'Appelle, French for "who calls," takes its name from an Indian legend of a young warrior who heard his dying lover call his name as he paddled his canoe across Katepwa Lake. So grief-stricken was he when told of her death that he drowned himself in the lake, and their voices are said to be heard in the wind that restlessly whips through the valley.

The heart of the valley is historic Fort Qu'Appelle. Short drives away are a restored 1869 Hudson's Bay Company fort at Last Mountain House, near the south end of Last Mountain Lake; North America's oldest bird sanctuary, established in 1887 further up the lake; the magnificently preserved Motherwell Homestead at Abernethy; and the striking Sacred Heart Church at Lebret, a francophone community on Katepwa, the largest of the five Fishing Lakes that run through the valley. To the southeast are Cannington Manor Historic Park and Moose Mountain Provincial Park.

Above: **Government House at Battleford.** *Top Right:* **As the sign says, this is Biggar.** *Bottom Right:* **Poundmaker's grave at Cut Knife Hill National Historic Site.** *Inset:* **Calf-roping during North Battleford's Northwest Territorial Days**

Historic Central Saskatchewan

Zone 3 is the parkland region of central Saskatchewan, with the North Saskatchewan River at its heart. In the centre of the zone is Battleford, once capital of the North-West Territories. History buffs can explore Fort Carlton and the battlefields at Batoche, where rifle pits dug by Métis rebels can still be seen in soft depressions in the grass, Fish Creek, Fort Pitt and Frenchman's Butte. At Cut Knife Hill, near where Chief Poundmaker sent Canadian soldiers packing, an 8000-kilogram (17 600-pound) tomahawk ("The World's Largest") has been erected as a symbol of unity and friendship.

The Eastern Parkland

Zone 4, includes the cities of Yorkton and Prince Albert as well as Blackstrap Provincial Park, with its artificial mountain built for the

1971 Canada Winter Games, and the heavily forested Duck Mountain Provincial Park on the Manitoba border. Just west of Duck Mountain, the National Doukhobour Heritage Village in the tiny town of Veregin, offers a glimpse of an often misunderstood culture.

A short drive north of Prince Albert is Prince Albert National Park, which covers some 400 000 hectares (nearly a million acres) of forested wilderness. Amid the park's spectacular scenery are found the cabin and gravesite of Grey Owl, the conservationist and author, who was a park ranger. Just outside the southeastern corner of the park is Emma Lake, an arts colony that draws artists and writers from around the country. A little further east, on Tobin Lake, lies Nipawin, known as "the northern pike capital of the world."

There are many other lakes in the region, the most interesting of which is probably Little Manitou Lake. Not only are its mineral-rich waters three times saltier than the ocean, but they are reputed to have medicinal powers. In fact, the early Plains Indians considered the lake sacred and called it the "Lake of Healing Waters."

Prince Albert National Park. *Inset:* **Grey Owl**

The Great Lone Land

Zone 5 is Saskatchewan's north, a land of 100 000 lakes. At Cumberland House, on the Saskatchewan River near the Manitoba border, visitors can enjoy views that have changed barely at all since the community — the oldest in the province — was first settled in 1774. At the northern tip of Highway 2, almost 800 kilometres (500 miles) from its beginning at the U.S. border, is La Ronge, a prime jumping-off point to the fishing and hunting country further north and home of an annual winter festival complete with dogsled and snowshoe races. A short drive north, on the Churchill River in Lac La Ronge Provincial Park, is Stanley Mission, with its magnificent Holy Trinity Anglican Church, the oldest building still standing in Saskatchewan. Further east at Pelican Narrows, paintings in red ochre that were left by Indians hundreds of years ago can still be seen on rock outcroppings. On the other side of the province and quite a bit further north is the great inland sea of Lake Athabasca, with vast stretches of rare sand dunes on one shore, and the all-but-abandoned remains of Uranium City, a mining town whose time has passed, perched on another.

Left: **Nistowiak Falls, on the Churchill River in Lac La Ronge Provincial Park.** *Below:* **Sand pillars more than 30 metres (100 feet) high rise above the Nipekamew River.**

Facts
at a Glance

General Information

Provincehood: September 1, 1905

Origin of Name: Saskatchewan comes from the Cree word *Kis-is-ski-tche-wan*, meaning "fast flowing water," and was first applied to the Saskatchewan River.

Provincial Capital: Regina

Provincial motto *Multis E Gentibus Vires:* "From many peoples strength"

Provincial Nickname: The Wheat Province

Provincial Flag: Equal horizontal bars of green (representing the northern forests) above and yellow (the prairies) below, with a prairie lily in the fly half and the shield of arms in the upper quarter on the staff side.

Coat of arms: Originally, three sheaves of golden wheat on a green background across a shield; above them, a red lion (representing the British Crown) against a field of gold. Adopted in 1906, this shield of arms was augmented in 1986 with a crest of a beaver and a crown above and a lion and a deer to either side. Below the shield is the provincial motto and a base of western red lilies.

Provincial tartan: Known officially as the Saskatchewan District Tartan. Its bold green and yellow squares, crossed by red lines, look much like the southern grain belt viewed from the air.

Provincial Bird: Prairie sharp-tailed grouse

Provincial Flower: Western red lily (also called the prairie lily)

Provincial Tree: White birch

Population

Population: 1 020 138 (April 1996), sixth among the provinces

(1991 census)
Population density: 1.73 per km^2 (2.8 per sq. mi.)

Population distribution: 63% of Saskatchewan residents live in cities or towns, 37% in the country, including 3.1% on Indian reserves.

Saskatoon	221 000
Regina	199 000
Prince Albert	34 181
Moose Jaw	33 593
Yorkton	15 314
Swift Current	14 815
North Battleford	14 350
Estevan	10 240
Weyburn	9 673

Lloydminster 7 241

* Melfort 5 628

Melville 4 905

* In Saskatchewan; another 10 042 live on the Alberta side of this border city

Population Growth:

Year	Population
1881	19 000
1901	91 279
1911	492 432
1921	757 510
1931	921 785
1941	895 992
1951	831 728
1961	925 181
1971	926 242
1981	968 313
1986	1 010 198
1991	988 928
1996	1 020 138

Geography

Borders: Saskatchewan lies between the 49th and 60th northern parallels of latitude and between 101° and 110° W longitude. It is bordered by the American states of North Dakota and Montana on the south, and by Alberta on the west, the Northwest Territories on the north, and Manitoba on the east. Saskatchewan is unique among the provinces in that all four borders are artificial and virtually straight.

Highest Point: Cypress Hills, 1468 m (4816 ft.)

Lowest Point: 213 m (699 ft.), along the shores of Lake Athabasca

Greatest Distance: North to south: 1225 km (761 mi.); east to west: 632 km (393 mi.) along the southern border.

Area:

Land surface: 570 700 km^2 (220 365 sq. mi.)

Water surface: 81 630 km^2 (31 520 sq. mi.)

Total: 652 330 km^2 (251 885 sq. mi.)

Rank in area among the provinces: Fifth

Rivers: Principal rivers are the South Saskatchewan, the North Saskatchewan, the Clearwater, the Churchill and the Qu'Appelle.

Lakes: There are about 100 000 lakes in Saskatchewan, most of them in the north. The largest are Lake Athabasca, about a third of which is in Alberta, and Reindeer Lake, which extends slightly into Manitoba. Other large lakes include Wollaston Lake, Cree Lake and Lac La Ronge.

Topography: Two-thirds of the province is prairie lowland, averaging 457 m to 610 m (1500 to 2000 ft.) above sea level; covered with deep fertile soil, the lowlands are exceptionally flat in some areas but elsewhere hummocky with many sloughs. The two branches of the Saskatchewan River cut across the lowlands. South of the river is a shallow, very flat, fertile brown-soil basin known as the Regina Plain. The northern third of the province is Canadian Shield, most of it covered with boreal forest and many lakes. In the south, the Missouri Coteau produces irregular terrain, with the Cypress Hills rising above this formation in the west.

National Parks: Prince Albert National Park, established in 1927 — 3874.6 km^2 (1496 sq. mi.); Grasslands, established 1981, still being formed.

Provincial parks: Duck Mountain, Cypress Hills, Moose Mountain and three others were created in 1931. There are now 31 provincial parks, including 9 historic parks, 11 natural parks, and a wilderness park. The rest (10) are recreational parks. Total developed area of parks: 9080 km^2 (3506 sq. mi.). There are also 21 protected areas, 8 historic sites and 152 recreation sites, and dozens of parks operated by 101 regional park authorities.

Climate: Southern Saskatchewan has a dry, sunny, continental climate with long, cold winters and hot summers. In the north, winters are exceptionally cold, the summers mild but rarely hot. Both regions experience all four seasons, and the south enjoys particularly fine autumns. Precipitation is low, averaging 275 mm to 500 mm (11 to 20 in.) on the plains, and the area is often subject to droughts. Frost-free days average around 100 in central Saskatchewan and up to 110 in the south. Average first frost is September 8, last May 25. Mean temperatures recorded at Regina are -17.9°C (0°F) in January, 18.9°C (66°F) in July. In the far north, winter temperatures are commonly in the -40s.

Time Zone: All of Saskatchewan lies within the Central Time Zone, though a few communities along the Alberta border use Mountain Time. Saskatchewan is the only province that doesn't use Daylight Saving Time.

Nature

Trees: 237 000 km^2 (91 500 sq. mi.) (almost 37% of total area) are forest. Among the native trees are aspen, white, black and balsam poplar, white and black spruce, jackpine and lodgepole pine (in the Cypress Hills only), birch, tamarack, willow, Manitoba maple, ash.

Wild Plants: Hundreds of varieties grow but those most commonly associated with Saskatchewan are saskatoon, with its delicious purple berries; chokecherry, with its mouth-puckering fruit; aromatic wolf willow, snowberry, prairie crocus, wild rose, cactus, and the prairie lily.

Animals: A few bison remain, but only in parks, and the grizzly bear is virtually gone; still abundant are pronghorn, elk, deer, moose, woodland caribou, black bear, mountain lion, lynx, timber wolf, coyote, beaver, muskrat, weasel, marten, fisher, hare, rabbit, ground squirrels, and red squirrel; the prairie dog, found nowhere else in Canada; and the swift fox, once extinct in the province. There are also nine species of snakes, of which the garter snake is the most common.

Birds: Birdwatchers have confirmed 349 species in Saskatchewan, of which

Wascana Centre

261 breed in the province. Upland game birds include the sharp-tailed grouse, Hungarian partridge, pheasant, ruffed grouse, and ptarmigan; waterfowl include the Canada goose, several varieties of duck, swans, grebes, the common loon, great blue heron, sandhill crane and almost extinct whooping crane, pelican, and a variety of sandpipers and gulls. In addition, there are crows, ravens, magpies, several species of woodpeckers, hawks and owls, including the endangered prairie falcon, ferruginous hawk and burrowing owl, along with a wide variety of songbirds

Fish: Common whitefish, tullibee, pickerel, yellow perch, small-mouth black bass, northern and walleyed pike, stickleback, goldeye, sturgeon, lake, brook and rainbow trout, grayling — 68 species in all. In addition, saline lakes of southern Saskatchewan produce a surprising catch: brine shrimp.

Insects: Too many to mention but three are worthy of note: mosquitoes and, in the north, black flies are hated pests; grasshoppers are pests that can seriously damage crops in years when their numbers are great.

Government

Provincial: Saskatchewan is a parliamentary democracy governed in the British style, with a Lieutenant-Governor, who represents the Crown, and a government made up of a premier, cabinet and legislative assembly. There are 66 seats in the legislative assembly.

Federal: Saskatchewan elects 14 members to the House of Commons and has six appointed Senators.

Local: Saskatchewan has 12 cities, 144 towns, 325 villages, 39 resort villages, 2 northern towns, 13 northern villages, 12 northern hamlets, 298 rural municipalities and 141 organized hamlets, for a total of 986 local governments.

Voting Qualifications: Voters must be Canadian citizens, 18 years or older and resident in Saskatchewan for at least six months.

Courts: A lower court, called the Provincial Court, looks after minor criminal offences and the early stages of major ones; an upper court, the Court of Queen's Bench, attends to cases involving serious crimes and civil suits. Appeals from either of these courts may be taken to the Saskatchewan Court of

Appeal, and, ultimately, to the Supreme Court of Canada. Judges of all three provincial courts are appointed by the federal government on the advice of the provincial justice minister.

Education

Education is compulsory for all children between the ages of 6 and 16. The province and local school districts jointly fund dual public and "separate" (Roman Catholic) systems running from kindergarten through grade 12, with 198 000 students and 12 500 teachers at 872 schools in 1995.

In addition, there are about 28 000 part-time and full-time students enrolled at the province's two universities, the University of Saskatchewan and the University of Regina. The Saskatchewan Institute of Applied Science and Technology enrolls another 15 000 full-time students and 35 000 part-timers at its four campuses. The Saskatchewan Indian Federated College in Regina, founded in 1976, has about 1000 students. It is the only Indian-controlled university-level college in the Americas.

The Economy

Superlatives: Saskatchewan produces 60% of Canada's wheat crop — around 12% of the world supply. It's the world's largest exporter of potash, producing a quarter of the world's supply. It's also the world's largest exporter of uranium, with about 25% of the world market. And it's the second-largest producer of oil in Canada.

Principal Products

Agriculture: Wheat, canola, barley, lentils, oats, beef, pork

Natural Resources: potash, uranium, oil, natural gas, coal, wood and wood pulp

Manufacturing: food products, beverages, steel, electronics

Business and trade: A quarter of all jobs are trade-related. About half of the province's products are exported, earning about $7 billion annually. The service-producing sector is the fastest growing and largest sector of the economy, accounting for over 300 000 jobs — two thirds of the total.

Tourism: Visitors spend around $900 million annually in Saskatchewan, and tourism is becoming increasingly important, providing 15 800 jobs.

Employment: About 450 000 people in Saskatchewan are employed. The unemployment rate, consistently the lowest in the country, was 6.0% in August 1996.

Social and Cultural Life

Music: Both Regina and Saskatoon have symphony orchestras, dance troupes and opera guilds. The Saskatchewan Music Festival Association sponsors around 50 festivals every spring, in which more than 50 000 Saskatchewan youngsters take part. There are also dozens of band and dance festivals for school children. Both universities have music

St. Elis Ukrainian Orthodox Church, Wroxton

departments, and the Regina Conservatory of Music, established in 1912, offers private lessons to children and adults. Music lovers can also enjoy a wide range of festivals during the summer months, from the Regina Folk Festival, Saskatoon's Jazz Festival and the Big Valley Jamboree to dozens of smaller ones.

Drama and Film: Saskatoon and Regina both have professional theatres, and Saskatoon stages an annual "fringe festival" in the summer. Drama is also popular in rural areas and there are 75 amateur theatre groups throughout the province. In Yorkton, the annual Short Film and Video Festival showcases up to 350 entries.

Museums and Galleries: Saskatchewan has about 300 public museums of all types. The most important are Regina's Royal Saskatchewan Museum and the RCMP Museum; Wanuskewin Heritage Park, just north of Saskatoon, with Native artifacts dating back 8000 years; and the Western Development Museums located in Saskatoon, Moose Jaw, Yorkton and North Battleford. Regina's MacKenzie Art Gallery and Saskatoon's Mendel Art Gallery have important permanent collections. There are many smaller museums and galleries throughout the province.

Libraries: Regina and Saskatoon both have excellent public libraries. The rest of the province is served by a regional library system providing service even to remote rural areas.

Sports and Recreation: The province has three professional sports teams — the Canadian Football League's Saskatchewan Roughriders and the Regina Cyclone and Saskatoon Riot of the Northern Baseball League. Junior and university football and other games are well attended, and large numbers of children take part at various levels in hockey, baseball and other sports.

Curling is a very popular winter activity, and Saskatchewan has produced several world champion rinks.

Saskatchewan people love fishing, camping, hiking, canoeing, white-water rafting and skiing, and take full advantage of the province's many park and recreation sites.

Historic Sites and Parks

Batoche National Historic Park, northeast of Saskatoon, has preserved the scene of the climactic battle of the

1885 Rebellion. The battlefield at Fish Creek and Fort Carlton Historic Park, with its reconstructed fur-trade-era buildings, are nearby.

Battleford National Historic Park is the site of a restored North-West Mounted Police post that figured in the 1885 Rebellion. Cut Knife Hill National Historic Site, scene of the battle between Poundmaker and Canadian forces, is nearby.

Cannington Manor Historic Park, in the southeast Moose Mountain area, is a restored 1890s-era village. The manor was an attempt to bring a bit of upper class England to the prairies, complete with polo and fox hunting.

Cumberland House Historic Park, at the site of the first inland Hudson Bay Company trading post, commemorates the oldest permanent settlement in the province.

Fort Pitt Provincial Historic Park, on the North Saskatchewan River near the Alberta border, is the site of a fur post dating back to 1829. The fort was besieged and abandoned during the 1885 Rebellion. Frenchman Butte Historic Site and Steele Narrows Provincial Historic Park, sites of other Rebellion skirmishes, are nearby.

Fort Walsh National Historic Park, in the Cypress Hills, was the first North-West Mounted Police post in the West; it has been restored to 1882 conditions. Nearby is restored Farwell's Post, site of the Cypress Hills Massacre of 1873.

Government House Historic Property, in Regina, was once the home of Lieutenant-Governors. Now restored and filled with antiques, the 100-year-old building is still used as an office by the Queen's representative.

Last Mountain House Provincial Historic Park, near Craven, features reconstructed buildings of the Hudson's Bay Company trading post.

Motherwell Homestead National Historic Park, at Abernethy, is a magnificently preserved field stone house, built in 1912 by farmer-politician W.R. Motherwell.

St. Victor's Petroglyphs Provincial Historic Park, site of an Indian holy place, contains centuries-old petroglyphs depicting Indian life.

Stanley Mission Provincial Historic Site, north of La Ronge and accessible by boat only, is home to the Holy Trinity Anglican Church. Built of squared timbers and adorned with stained glass brought from England in the 1850s, it is

Blacksmith shop in the Saskatoon Western Development Museum's 1910 Boomtown

the oldest building still standing in the province.

Wood Mountain Post Provincial Historic Park, close to the U.S. border in the southwest, marks the place where Sitting Bull and his Sioux followers camped after defeating General Custer at Little Bighorn.

Other Interesting Places to Visit

Allen Sapp Gallery, in North Battleford, features many paintings by the renowned Cree artist. It is also an interpretive centre offering insight into the way of life of the Cree.

John G. Diefenbaker Centre, on the University of Saskatchewan campus, showcases memorabilia of the 13th prime minister. Diefenbaker and his wife are buried nearby.

The Legislative Building, in Regina's Wascana Centre, is the seat of government for the province. The imposing cross-shaped, black-domed building, clad in Tyndall stone, opened in 1912.

Manitou Beach has long been known for the restorative powers of the mineral waters in briny Little Manitou Lake, which has a density like that of the Dead Sea.

National Doukhobour Heritage Village, in Veregin, provides a glimpse of the way of life of the Russian religious refugees who settled in the area in 1899.

Pelican Narrows, northwest of Flin Flon, Manitoba, is the jumping off spot for viewing Indian rock art, found at 21 locations along the Churchill River system. The red ochre paintings left by Indians hundreds of years ago are protected as heritage properties.

Prince Albert National Park, with over 400 000 ha (nearly a million acres) of forested wilderness, contains some spectacular scenery, as well as the cabin and gravesite of Grey Owl.

RCMP Centennial Museum and Chapel, in Regina, on the site of the

Megamunch, the Royal Saskatchewan Museum's moving, roaring, half-size Tyrannosaurus Rex

force's training academy. In the summer, the pomp and pageantry of the force's early days are recaptured by the Sergeant Major's Parade and the Sunset Retreat Ceremony.

Royal Saskatchewan Museum, formerly known as the *Museum of Natural History*, in Regina, was built in 1955 to commemorate the province's fiftieth anniversary. Children are fascinated by its lifelike dioramas and especially by Megamunch, the growling, head-shaking Tyrannosaurus Rex.

Wanuskewin Heritage Park, just north of Saskatoon, is an archaeological treasure, where Native artifacts dating back 8000 years have been found and are on display in natural settings.

Western Development Museum, in Saskatoon, documents the history of the province's pioneer life. A highlight is the main street of Boomtown 1910. There are also branches of the museum in Moose Jaw, Yorkton and North Battleford.

Wanuskewin, a 100-hectare (290-acre) heritage park located just outside Saskatoon, opened in 1992. The Northern Plains Indians of prehistory visited the Wanuskewin area on a regular basis for 8000 years. Archaeologists have identified 21 habitation, bison kill and other sites within the park, which also features reconstructed encampments, an outdoor amphitheatre and an exhibit hall where the culture of the Northern Plains Indians is interpreted for visitors.

Important Dates

1670   The Hudson's Bay Company obtains title to Rupert's Land

1690   Henry Kelsey is the first European in Saskatchewan

1741   Pierre Gaultier de Varennes, sieur de La Vérendrye, builds Fort Bourbon on the South Saskatchewan River

1774   Cumberland House, the first permanent settlement in what is now Saskatchewan, is established by Samuel Hearne

1840   The first school is established, by missionary Henry Budd, at Cumberland House

1867   The Dominion of Canada is created

1870   The Dominion of Canada officially takes possession of Rupert's Land and reorganizes the bulk of it as the North-West Territories

1872   Parliament enacts the Dominion Lands Act

1873   A group of Assiniboine are killed in what becomes known as the Cypress Hills Massacre; the incident speeds establishment of the North-West Mounted Police

1874   Cree and Ojibwa sign Treaty Number 4 in southern Saskatchewan; subsequent treaties are signed with the Plains and Wood Cree of central Saskatchewan in 1876, and with Chipewyan and Cree of northeastern Saskatchewan in 1906

1875   The Mounted Police establish Fort Walsh at Cypress Hills

1876   Battleford is selected as capital of the North-West Territories

1878   The first public school is opened in Battleford; the first newspaper, Battleford's *Saskatchewan Herald*, begins publishing

1882   The Canadian Pacific Railway comes through Saskatchewan

1883   The capital of the North-West Territories is moved to Regina

1884   A group of white and Métis settlers invite Louis Riel to negotiate on their behalf with the federal government

1885   Government troops put down the Northwest Rebellion; Riel surrenders, is convicted of treason and hanged

1905   Saskatchewan becomes a province; Liberal Walter Scott is first premier

1909   Saskatoon is selected as site of University of Saskatchewan;

1912   Part of downtown Regina is destroyed by a tornado

1916   Saskatchewan women win the vote

1924   Farmers organize the Saskatchewan Wheat Pool

1925   Prime Minister William Lyon Mackenzie King, having lost his Ontario seat, runs in a Prince Albert by-election and wins

1929   Conservative J.T.M. Anderson becomes premier

1930   The federal government transfers control of Saskatchewan's natural resources to the province

1931	Net farm income drops drastically; police and striking coal miners clash in Estevan
1933	The newly formed Co-Operative Commonwealth Federation issues the Regina Manifesto
1935	The On-to-Ottawa Trek stalls in Regina and ends in a riot in which one policeman is killed, 82 people injured
1937	Worst drought on record; legislation allowing credit unions is enacted; sales tax, at 2%, is introduced
1944	The CCF wins a massive victory; Tommy Douglas becomes premier
1947	The Saskatchewan Hospitalization Plan goes into effect
1948	The Saskatchewan Arts Board is created to foster the arts
1951	Oil is struck at Roseray No. 1, the first producing well in Saskatchewan
1953	Uranium production begins
1957	Saskatchewan lawyer John Diefenbaker becomes prime minister
1961	Tommy Douglas is elected national leader of the CCF's successor, the New Democratic Party
1962	Doctors strike over Medicare; continuous production of potash begins
1964	The Liberal Party under Ross Thatcher squeaks to victory
1967	The Gardiner Dam is completed, creating Lake Diefenbaker
1969	The Saskatchewan Indian and Métis department is created

	— the first such provincial government department in Canada
1971	The NDP's Allan Blakeney becomes premier
1974	The University of Regina gains autonomy as a separate institution
1982	Conservative Grant Devine becomes premier
1991	Roy Romanow leads the NDP to victory
1995	NDP eliminates deficit, wins re-election

Big Bear

M.J. Coldwell

Nicholas Flood Davin

John G. Diefenbaker

Important People

Big Bear (c.1825-1888), Cree chief, born near Fort Carlton; was reluctant to get involved in the Northwest Rebellion, but his band was responsible for the attack at Frog Lake and fought last battle of the Rebellion at Frenchman's Butte; served two years in prison for treason

Archie Belaney, a.k.a. Grey Owl (1888-1938); English-born conservationist and author, in Canada from age 17; he created the hoax of the Indian Grey Owl, writing several highly popular books and lecturing under that name; appointed park ranger at Prince Albert National Park, where he is buried

Paul Brodie (1934-   ), born and raised in Regina; saxophone virtuoso; has recorded more than three dozen albums and performed in over 2500 shows all over the world

Maria Campbell (1940-   ), born in Batoche area; Métis writer; her autobiographical *Halfbreed,* recounting her struggle to survive a life on the streets, was important in the revival of Native culture in the 1970s; author of many other books, plays and radio plays

Ethel Catherwood (1909-1987); high jumper; raised and trained in Saskatoon; nicknamed "The Saskatoon Lily," she won the gold medal in the women's high jump in the 1928 Olympics and remains the only Canadian woman to win an individual gold medal in Olympic track and field

M.J. Coldwell (1888-1974); English-born teacher, politician; one of the founders of the Co-Operative Commonwealth Federation in 1932; Member of Parliament 1935-58 and leader of national CCF 1942-60

Lorna Crozier (1948-   ), born in Swift Current; author of eight books, she is fast becoming one of Canada's best-known poets

Nicholas Flood Davin (1843-1901), Irish-born newspaperman, politician; founded the Regina *Leader*, the city's first newspaper, in 1883; elected to Parliament as a Conservative in 1887

Edgar Dewdney (1835-1916); British-born surveyor, politician; a Conservative member of Parliament from British Columbia, he was appointed Indian commissioner of North-West Territories in 1879 and Lieutenant-Governor in 1881, serving in both capacities until 1888

John G. Diefenbaker (1895-1979); lawyer and politician; raised on a Saskatchewan homestead; practised law in Prince Albert and was leader of

Saskatchewan Conservative Party in the 1938 election; elected to Parliament in 1940; became federal Conservative leader in 1956 and prime minister the following year; massively re-elected in 1958; leader of the Opposition 1963-67

Tommy Douglas (1904-1986); Scottish-born Baptist minister, politician; one of the founders of the CCF, he served two terms in Parliament before becoming leader of the Saskatchewan party in 1942; led the party to victory in 1944 and implemented ground-breaking social reforms during his 17 years as premier; became national leader of the NDP in 1961 and served in Parliament until 1979

Gabriel Dumont (1837-1906); born at Red River; buffalo hunter, political and military leader; led the Métis forces at Batoche during the Northwest Rebellion of 1885; given political refuge in the U.S., he toured with Buffalo Bill's Wild West Show before eventually coming back to Saskatchewan

Joe Fafard (1942-   ); born at Ste-Marthe; sculptor; his plaster, clay and bronze figures of people and animals — particularly cows — have won him an international audience

Sylvia Fedoruk (1927-   ); born in Canora; nuclear physicist; was a professor, researcher and pioneer in the use of radiation therapy for 35 years at the Saskatoon Cancer Clinic; served as Lieutenant-Governor in 1988-1994, first woman to hold the post in Saskatchewan

Frederick W.G. Haultain (1857-1942); lawyer, politician, judge; premier of the North-West Territories legislative assembly (1897-1905), he was leading advocate of provincehood for the Territories; leader of the Opposition from 1905 until 1912; chief justice of Saskatchewan 1917-1938

Ramon John Hnatyshyn (1934-   ); born in Saskatoon; lawyer, politician, Governor General of Canada; Member of Parliament from 1974 to 1988, he served in several cabinet positions, including that of justice minister; served as Governor General in 1989-1994

Gordie Howe (1928-   ); born in Floral; hockey player; played 26 seasons with the NHL Detroit Red Wings and 6 seasons with World Hockey Association teams; broke many NHL scoring records and won the Hart Trophy for most valuable player 6 times; still holds NHL record for most seasons and most regular season games played

Frances Hyland (1927-   ); born in Shaunavon; actress; trained

Gabriel Dumont

Sylvia Fedoruk

Ramon Hnatyshyn

Gordie Howe

Frances Hyland

Connie Kaldor

Augustus Kenderdine

Andrew McNaughton

in London, England, she began her stage career there in 1950; a regular at the Stratford Shakespearean Festival, she has also appeared on Broadway, in films and on television

Colin James (1964-   ); born in Regina; popular blues singer-guitarist; became a hit national recording artist in the late eighties, winning two Junos in 1991

Connie Kaldor (1953-   ); born in Regina; Juno-winning singer-songwriter with many records: one of Canada's best and best-known folk singers

Henry Kelsey (c.1667-1724); fur trader and explorer; an employee of the Hudson's Bay Company, he explored the West in 1690-91, encouraging Indians to trade with the company; is the first European known to have set foot in Saskatchewan

Augustus F. Kenderdine (1870-1947); British-born painter, educator; joined the University of Saskatchewan as art lecturer in 1927; started the Emma Lake Summer School of Art 1935; moved to Regina College, establishing a school of art there in 1936

Ron Lancaster (1938-   ), Pennsylvania-born football player, coach; one of the best quarterbacks in CFL history, he led the Saskatchewan Roughriders from 1963 to 1978,

making the championships five times and winning one Grey Cup; served as coach for the 1979 and 1980 seasons

Franklin Laubach (1856-1923); musician; founding conductor Regina Philharmonic Society, formed in 1904; organized Saskatchewan Music Festival Association in 1908

Ernest Lindner (1897-1988); Austrian-born artist; came to Saskatchewan in 1926 as a farm labourer; taught at the Saskatchewan Technical Institute 1936-62, with many summers at Emma Lake Summer School of Art

Kenneth Lochhead (1926-   ); Ottawa-born abstract painter; member of the influential Regina Five, he was head of the Regina College School of Art through the fifties

Edward McCourt (1907-1972); writer, educator; author of five novels set in the prairie landscape and several works of non-fiction; as an English professor at the University of Saskatchewan, he championed the study of Canadian literature

Norman MacKenzie (1869-1934); Regina lawyer and art patron; left his art collection to Regina College on his death

Jean Ethel MacLachlan (1875-1963), Nova Scotia-born teacher, social worker; appointed juvenile court judge in 1917, she was the first woman judge in Saskatchewan

Andrew McNaughton (1887-1966); born at Moosomin; army officer, scientist and diplomat; after service in the First World War, joined the permanent force and rose rapidly to become chief of the general staff; was commander of the Canadian forces in the Second World War; later, he represented Canada at the United Nations and served on several international boards and commissions

Violet McNaughton (1879-1968); teacher, journalist, suffragist; a founder of the women's section of the Saskatchewan Grain Growers, she led the women's suffrage movement in the province and then continued to campaign for changes that would improve the lives of women and children

Eli Mandel (1922-1992); born in Estevan; poet, critic and university professor; author of over 10 books of poetry; winner of the Governor-General's Award for poetry in 1967 for *An Idiot Joy*

Reuben Mayes (1964-   ), born in North Battleford; football player; after an outstanding college career with Washington State, during which he set a collegiate rushing record of 357 yards in a single game, became a

star running back with the National Football League's New Orleans Saints; 1986 rookie of the year

Fred S. Mendel (1888-1976); industrialist, art patron; founded Intercontinental Packers in Saskatoon in 1937; donated money and art for the Mendel Art Gallery

Joni Mitchell (1943-   ); raised in Saskatoon, now living in U.S.; popular singer/songwriter; her folk- and jazz-oriented pop songs, such as "Both Sides Now" and "Woodstock," have made her an international star

W.O. Mitchell (1914-   ); born in Weyburn; writer; transformed his hometown into "Crocus, Saskatchewan," in his first novel, *Who Has Seen the Wind*, a Canadian classic; other novels, stories and plays have made him one of Canada's most popular writers

Hilda Neatby (1904-1975); grew up in Saskatchewan; historian, educator; taught for many years at the University of Saskatchewan, but is best known for her controversial book *So Little for the Mind* criticizing Canada's educational system

W.J. Patterson (1886-1976); born at Grenfell; politician, first Saskatchewan-born premier; served as Liberal leader and premier from 1935 to 1944 and as

Violet McNaughton

Reuben Mayes

W.O. Mitchell

Hilda Neatby

Poundmaker

Louis Riel

Sinclair Ross

Buffy Sainte-Marie

Lieutenant-Governor 1951-58; the first person in Saskatchewan to hold both top posts

Poundmaker (1826-1886); Saskatchewan-born Cree chief; a peacemaker among Indian tribes and one of the negotiators of Treaty 6; at Cut Knife Hill during the Northwest Rebellion, he held his men back, allowing the government troops to retreat and preventing a probable slaughter; sentenced to three years in prison but released after nine months

Sarah Ramsland (1882-1964); Minnesota-born teacher, librarian; first woman elected to Saskatchewan legislature 1919; a Liberal, she was re-elected in 1921

George Reed (1939-   ); Mississippi-born football player; an outstanding fullback with the Saskatchewan Roughriders 1962-75, he set 44 Canadian Football League records; active in charitable work including the George Reed Foundation for the Handicapped

Ernie Richardson (1931-   ); born in Stoughton; curling champion; his Saskatchewan rink was perhaps the best in Canadian history, winning the Brier and the international championship Scotch Cup four times in five years between 1959 and 1963

Louis Riel (1844-1885); born at Red River; Métis leader; set up a provisional government at Red River in 1869 and forced the entry of Manitoba into Confederation as a province; after 15 years of exile in the U.S., he returned to Canada to lead the Saskatchewan Métis, sparking the Northwest Rebellion of 1885; hanged for treason in Regina

Sinclair Ross (1908-   ); born at Shellbrook; writer; his novel *As for Me and My House*, published in 1941, is a Canadian classic; retired from a lifelong banking career in 1968, moving to Greece and Spain before returning to Canada in 1980

Buffy Sainte-Marie (1941-   ); born on Piapot Reserve; singer-songwriter; became an important figure on New York folk music scene in the 1960s; her rich, vibrant voice, strong social commentaries in songs such as "The Universal Soldier," and love ballads like "Until It's Time for You To Go" made her an international star

Allen Sapp (1929-   ); born on Red Pheasant Reserve; painter; his oil renditions of Plains Cree life of the 1930s and 40s have earned him a reputation as one of Canada's foremost painters

Andy Suknaski (1942-   ); born at Wood Mountain; poet; a master of the narrative, vernacular style, his 1976 volume *Wood Mountain Poems* is one of the most influential books in contemporary Canadian poetry

Guy Vanderhaeghe (1951-   ); born in Esterhazy; writer; highly successful short story writer and novelist, his first collection of stories, *Man Descending,* won the Governor General's Award in 1982

Peter Verigin (1859-1924); Russian-born religious leader; spiritual and political leader of 7400 Doukhobours who immigrated to Saskatchewan in 1899; in 1908, he led many of them to B.C. when land granted to them in Saskatchewan was taken back because they refused to take an oath of allegiance

Jon Vickers (1926-   ); born in Prince Albert; singer; has performed in all the great opera houses of the world and is considered one of the finest dramatic tenors of the late twentieth century

Dr. Stephen Worobetz (1914-   ); born in Krydor; surgeon; became the province's 13th Lieutenant-Governor in 1970; was the first person of Ukrainian descent and first one born in the province to hold post

Peter Verigin

Dr. Stephen Worobetz

Premiers of Saskatchewan

Walter Scott	Liberal	1905-16
William M. Martin	Liberal	1916-22
Charles A. Dunning	Liberal	1922-26
James G. Gardiner	Liberal	1926-29
James T. M. Anderson	Conservative	1929-34
James G. Gardiner	Liberal	1934-35
William J. Patterson	Liberal	1935-44
Thomas C. Douglas	CCF	1944-61
Woodrow S. Lloyd	CCF/NDP	1961-64
W. Ross Thatcher	Liberal	1964-71
Allen E. Blakeney	NDP	1971-82
Grant Devine	Progressive Conservative	1982-91
Roy Romanow	NDP	1991-

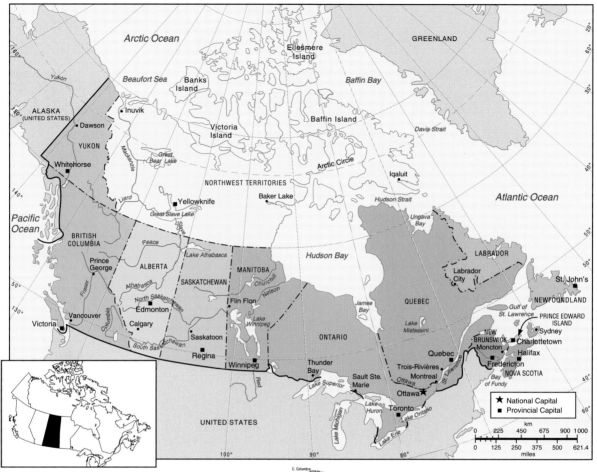

Arctic Ocean

GREENLAND

Ellesmere
Island

Yukon

Beaufort Sea

Banks
Island

Baffin Bay

ALASKA
(UNITED STATES)

Inuvik

Victoria
Island

Baffin Island

Dawson

Davis Strait

YUKON

Great
Bear Lake

Whitehorse

Arctic Circle

Iqaluit

Liard

NORTHWEST TERRITORIES

Atlantic Ocean

Mackenzie

Yellowknife

Baker Lake

Hudson Strait

Pacific
Ocean

Great Slave Lake

Ungava
Bay

LABRADOR

BRITISH
COLUMBIA

Peace

Lake Athabasca

Hudson Bay

Labrador
City

Prince
George

ALBERTA

SASKATCHEWAN

MANITOBA

Churchill

St. John's

Fraser

Athabasca

North Saskatchewan

Flin Flon

Nelson

QUEBEC

NEWFOUNDLAND

Edmonton

James
Bay

Lake
Mistassini

PRINCE EDWARD
ISLAND

Columbia

Vancouver

Calgary

Lake
Winnipeg

Gulf of
St. Lawrence

Sydney

Victoria

South Sas.

Saskatoon

ONTARIO

NEW
BRUNSWICK

Charlottetown

Saskatchewan

Regina

Winnipeg

Thunder
Bay

Moncton

Halifax

Quebec

Fredericton

NOVA SCOTIA

Red

Trois-Rivières

Montreal

St. Lawrence

Bay
of Fundy

Sault Ste.
Marie

Ottawa

Lake Superior

Ottawa

★ National Capital

■ Provincial Capital

Lake
Huron

Toronto

km

Lake Michigan

UNITED STATES

Lake Ontario

0 225 450 675 900 1000

Lake Erie

0 125 250 375 500 621.4

miles

Topography

© Hammond Inc., Maplewood, N.J.

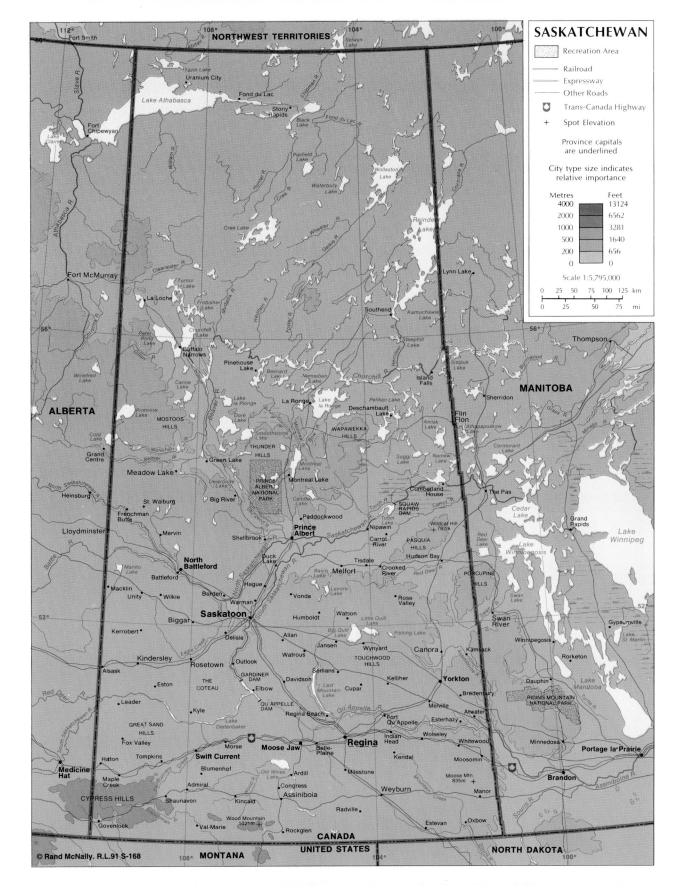

SASKATCHEWAN

Recreation Area
Railroad
Expressway
Other Roads
Trans-Canada Highway
Spot Elevation

Province capitals
are underlined

City type size indicates
relative importance

Metres	Feet
4000	13124
2000	6562
1000	3281
500	1640
200	656
0	0

Scale 1:5,795,000

0 25 50 75 100 125 km
0 25 50 75 mi

NORTHWEST TERRITORIES

Fort Smith
Uranium City
Tazin Lake
Fond du Lac
Stony Rapids
Black Lake
Lake Athabasca
Fort Chipewyan
Lake Claire
Selwyn Lake
Chipman R.
Fond du Lac R.
Pasfield Lake
Wollaston Lake
Waterbury Lake
Cree R.
Harper R.
Wheeler R.
Geikie R.
Cree Lake
Reindeer Lake
Lynn Lake
William R.
Athabasca R.
Firebag R.
Clearwater R.
Fort McMurray
Turnor Lake
La Loche
Frobisher Lake
Mudjatik R.
Churchill Lake
Peter Pond Lake
Dillon R.
Buffalo Narrows
Pinehouse Lake
Besnard Lake
Nemeiben Lake
Churchill R.
Island Falls
Sisipuk Lake
Burntwood R.
Thompson
MANITOBA
Winefred Lake
Primrose Lake
Canoe Lake
Beaver R.
Smoothstone Lake
Deschambault Lake
Pelikan Lake
Steephill Lake
Reindeer R.
Sherridon
Grass R.
Cold Lake
ALBERTA
MOSTOOS HILLS
Dore Lake
La Ronge
Lake la Ronge
WAPAWEKKA HILLS
Amisk Lake
Flin Flon
Athapapuskow Lake
Namew Lake
Cormorant Lake
Grand Centre
Waterhen R.
Green Lake
THUNDER HILLS
Smoothstone Lake
PRINCE ALBERT NATIONAL PARK
Montreal Lake
Suggi Lake
Saskatchewan R.
Minago R.
Meadow Lake
Delaronde Lake
Montreal Lake
Cumberland House
The Pas
Cedar Lake
Heinsburg
North Saskatchewan R.
Big River
Candle Lake
SQUAW RAPIDS DAM
Carrot R.
Lake Winnipegosis
St. Walburg
Sturgeon R.
Paddockwood
Tobin Lake
Wildcat Hill +782m
Red Deer R.
Grand Rapids
Frenchman Butte
Shellbrook
Nipawin
PASQUIA HILLS
Lake Winnipeg
Lloydminster
Mervin
Duck Lake
Prince Albert
Carrot River
Hudson Bay
Battle R.
North Battleford
Hague
South Saskatchewan R.
Tisdale
Crooked River
Red Deer R.
PORCUPINE HILLS
Battleford
Borden
Basin Lake
Melfort
Swan R.
Swan Lake
Manito Lake
Warman
Vonda
Lenore Lake
Rose Valley
Swan River
Gypsumville
Macklin
Unity
Wilkie
Humboldt
Watson
Little Quill Lake
Winnipegosis
Lake St. Martin
Saskatoon
Biggar
Kerrobert
Delisle
Allan
Jansen
Wynyard
Fishing Lake
Kamsack
Big Quill Lake
Rorketon
Watrous
TOUCHWOOD HILLS
Canora
Dauphin
Kindersley
Rosetown
Outlook
Davidson
Semans
Kelliher
Yorkton
Lake Manitoba
RIDING MOUNTAIN NATIONAL PARK
Alsask
Eston
GARDINER DAM
Elbow
Last Mountain Lake
Cupar
Bredenbury
Eagle Creek
THE COTEAU
Leader
Kyle
QU'APPELLE DAM
Regina Beach
Qu'Appelle R.
Melville
Atwater
Turtle R.
Red Deer R.
Lake Diefenbaker
Fort Qu'Appelle
Esterhazy
Minnedosa
GREAT SAND HILLS
Morse
Belle Plaine
Regina
Indian Head
Wolseley
Whitewood
Moosomin
Portage la Prairie
Fox Valley
Moose Jaw
Kendal
Brandon
Hatton
Tompkins
Swift Current
Blumenhof
Ardill
Congress
Milestone
Weyburn
Moose Mtn. 835m +
Manor
Assiniboine R.
Medicine Hat
Maple Creek
Admiral
Kincaid
Assiniboia
Radville
Souris R.
CYPRESS HILLS
Shaunavon
Wood Mountain 1021m +
Rockglen
Estevan
Oxbow
Govenlock
Val-Marie
Old Wives Lake
CANADA
MONTANA
UNITED STATES
NORTH DAKOTA

© Rand McNally. R.L.91 S-168

AVERAGE ANNUAL RAINFALL

All of Saskatchewan receives less than 18 inches—455 mm—of rain a year, most of it during the summer months.

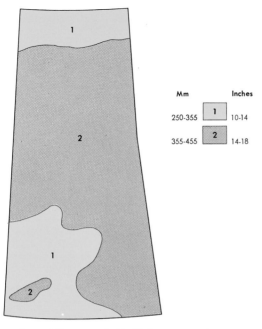

Mm		Inches
250-355	1	10-14
355-455	2	14-18

Figures within areas are for identification purposes only.

GROWING SEASON

There is a growing season of three months or less in much of Saskatchewan.

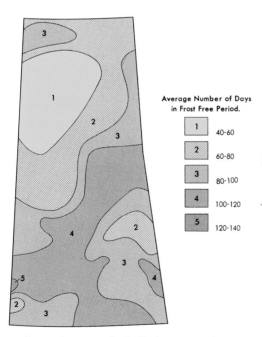

Average Number of Days in Frost Free Period.

1	40-60
2	60-80
3	80-100
4	100-120
5	120-140

Figures within areas are for identification purposes only.

ECONOMY

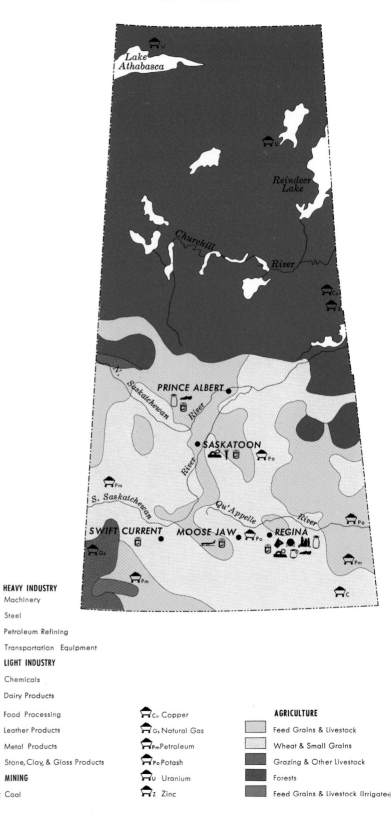

HEAVY INDUSTRY
- Machinery
- St Steel
- Petroleum Refining
- Transportation Equipment

LIGHT INDUSTRY
- Chemicals
- Dairy Products
- Food Processing
- Leather Products
- Metal Products
- Stone, Clay, & Glass Products

MINING
- c Coal

- Cu Copper
- Gs Natural Gas
- Pm Petroleum
- Po Potash
- U Uranium
- z Zinc

AGRICULTURE
- Feed Grains & Livestock
- Wheat & Small Grains
- Grazing & Other Livestock
- Forests
- Feed Grains & Livestock (Irrigated)

Index

Page numbers that appear in boldface type indicate illustrations

Abernethy, 100
agriculture, 17, 51-52, 55-56, 64, 73-76, 109, 124
Americans, 18, 49
Anglicans, 21, 33, 34
animals, 14-15, 107
area, 9, 106
arts, 23-24, 83-89
Assiniboine, 22, 23, 25, 30, 34
Austrians, 53
Balgonie, 45
Barr colonists, **48**
Barr, Isaac, 48
Batoche, 36, 38, 39, 101, 110-11
Batoche, Battle of, **40,** 40-41
Battleford, 35, 37, 38, 41, 70, 101, 111
Belaney, Archie. *See* Grey Owl
Bienfait, 100
Big Bear, 37, 39, 40, 42, **116,** 116
Big Muddy Badlands, **11,** 99
Big Valley Jamboree, 88-89, 110
Biggar, **101**
bird, provincial, **104,** 105
birds, 15, 100, 107-8
Blackfoot, 23, 27
Blackstrap Provincial Park, 101
Blakeney, Allan, 63
Bloore, Ron, 87
borders, 28, 34, 48, 106
British Commonwealth Air Training Plan, 57
Britons, 18, 19, 20, 36-37, 47, 49, 52
Brodie, Paul, 116
Budd, Henry, 70
buffalo, 14-15, 23, 25-26, **26,** 30, 35, 77, 107
Butala, Sharon, 85
Campbell, Maria, 116
Canadian Northern, 49
Canadian Pacific Railway, 18, 35, 37, 49, 114
Canadian Shield, 12, 12, 107
Cannington Manor, 36-37, **46,**

100, 111
canola, **72,** 73
Canora, 20
caribou, 15, 23, 26
Catherwood, Ethel, **91,** 116
Catholics, 20, 33, 38, 71
Chautauqua, 55
Churchill River, 13, 106
Cicansky, Vic, 87
Clearwater River, 106
climate, 14, 107
Co-operative Commonwealth Federation, 59-62, 80
coal, 78
coat of arms, **104,** 105
Coldwell, M.J., **116,** 116
Conservative party, 64, 73
courts, 68, 108-9
Craven, 88
Cree, 20, 23, 27, 30, 39, 41, 42
Cree Lake, 13, 106
Crozier, L.W.F., 38, 39
Crozier, Lorna, 116
Cumberland House, 29, 70, 103, 111
curling, 91, 110
Cut Knife Hill, 41, **101,** 101, 111
cyclone of 1912, 50, **51**
Cypress Hills, 98, 106, 107
Cypress Hills Massacre, 34, 98, 111
Danes, 45
Davin, Nicholas Flood, **46, 116,** 116
Dene, 23, 26
Devine, Grant, 64, 73
Dewdney, Edgar, 116
Diefenbaker, John G., 63, 96, 97-98, 112, 115, **116,** 116-17
dinosaurs, 10, 98, **112**
Dirt Hills, 35
doctors' strike, 61, 62
Dominion Lands Act, 34
Douglas, Tommy, 59, **60,** 63, 117
Doukhobours, 47, 53, 102
drought, **55,** 55-56, 73, 115
Duck Lake, Battle of, 38
Duck Mountain Provincial Park, 102, 107

Dumont, Gabriel, 38-41, **117,** 117
Ebenezer, 45
economy, 25-27, 60-64, 72-81, 109, 124
Edenbridge, 45
education, 33, 70-71, 109
Emma Lake Summer School of Art, 86, 102
environment, 64
Esterhazy, 45
Estevan, 56, 100
Fafard, Joe, 83, 87, 117
Federation of Saskatchewan Indian Nations, 31
Fedoruk, Sylvia, **117,** 117
festivals, 19-20, 20, 85-86, 88
Finns, 18
First World War, 52-53
fish, 79, 89, 108
Fish Creek, 101, 111
Fish Creek, Battle of, **32,** 39-40
flag, **104,** 105
flower, provincial, **104,** 105
Foam Lake, 45
Folk, Rick, 91
forest, 9, 12, 15, 79, 107
Fort Battleford, **93**
Fort Carlton, 101, 111
Fort Paskoyac, 29
Fort Pitt, 39, 101, 111
Fort Qu'Appelle, 83, 100
Fort Walsh, 98, **99,** 111, 114
francophones, 20, 47, 71, 88
Frenchman's Butte, 42, 101, 111
Frog Lake, 39
fur trade, 28-30, 79
Gardiner Dam, **63**
Gardiner, James, 63
Gault, Connie, 85
geography, 9-14, 98-103, 106-7
Germans, 18, 19, 20, 45, 47, 53
Globe Theatre, 85, 96
Godwin, Ted, 87
government, 46, 66-69, 108-9
Grand Trunk Pacific, 49
grasslands. *See* prairie
Grasslands National Park, **24,** 90, 99, 107
Gravelbourg, 48

Great Depression, 18, 55-57
Great Sand Hills, **11,** 98-99
Grey Owl, **102,** 102, 116
Gros Ventre, 23, 27
Hart Rouge, **88,** 89
Haultain, F.W.G., 46, 48, 49, 117
Haverstock, Linda, 64
Hearne, Samuel, 29
highways, 80
Hind, Henry, 33
historic sites, 110-12
Hnatyshyn, Ramon, **117,** 117
Holy Trinity Anglican Church,
 34, 103, 111
Howe, Gordie, **117,** 117
Hudson's Bay Company, 28-29,
 33
Humboldt, 20
Hungarians, 45, 47
hunting, 25-27, **26,** 89
Hyland, Frances, 117-18, **118**
Ice Age, 10, 98
Icelanders, 20, 45
immigration, 18, 19, 45-49, **48, 50**
Indians, 18, 19, 20, 23-31, 35, 37,
 38-43, 48, 102, 113, 114
insects, 108
James, Colin, 89, 118
Jews, 21, 45
Kaldor, Connie, **118,** 118
Kelsey, Henry, 17, 114, 118
Kenderdine, Augustus, 86, **118,**
 118
Kerr, Illingworth, 87
Knowles, Dorothy, 83, 86, 87
Kramer, Ken and Sue, 85
Ku Klux Klan, 54
La Vérendrye, 29, 114
Lac La Ronge, 13, 106
 Provincial Park, **103,** 103
Lake Athabasca, 13, 103, 106
Lake Diefenbaker, 13, 99
lakes, 13, 106
Lancaster, Ron, 90, 118
Langham, **21**
languages, 20, 23
Last Mountain House, 100, 111
Laubach, Frank, 87, 88, 118
Laurier, Sir Wilfrid, 47, 48, 49
Lebret, 100
Legislative Building, 50, **66,** 96,

112
Liberal party, 49, 52, 62, 64
Lindner, Ernest, 118
Little Manitou Lake, 102, 112
Lloyd, G.E., 48
Lloyd, Woodrow, 61, 62
Lloydminster, 19, 48, 78
Lochhead, Kenneth, 86, 87, 118
lotteries, 83
McCourt, Edward, 84, 118
Macdonald, Sir John A., 34, 42
MacKenzie Art Gallery, 86, 87,
 96
MacKenzie, Norman, 86, 118
MacLachlan, Jean, 118-19
McNaughton, Andrew, 57, **118,**
 119
McNaughton, Violet, 53, **119,** 119
Macoun, John, 37
Mandel, Eli, 83, 84, 119
manufacturing, 79, 109
Maple Creek, 37, 99
maps of Canada
 political, **122**
 topographical, **122**
maps of Saskatchewan
 growing season, **124**
 political, **123**
 precipitation, **124**
 principal products, **124**
Mayes, Reuben, **119,** 119
Medicare, 60, 61-62, 63, 71
Melville, 19
Mendel Art Gallery, **86,** 87, 97
Mendel, Fred S., 86-87, 119
Mennonites, 21, 47, 53
Métis, 17-18, 31, 34, 36, 37, 38-43
Middleton, Frederick Dobson,
 39-41, **41**
mines and minerals, 61, 63, 76-77
Mitchell, Joni, 89, 119
Mitchell, Ken, 85
Mitchell, Marge, 91
Mitchell, W.O., 7, 83, 84, **119,** 119
Moose Jaw, 37, 54, 57, 89, 92, **99**
Moose Mountain Provincial
 Park, 100, 107
Motherwell Homestead, **100,** 111
motto, 105
municipalities, 68, 108
Museum of Natural History. *See*

Royal Saskatchewan Museum
museums and galleries, 86-87,
 89, 110, 112-13
music, 70, 87-89, 109-10
names and nicknames, 7, 105
Native people, 17-20, 22-31, 89.
 See also Indians; Métis
Neatby, Hilda, **119,** 119
New Democratic Party, 61-62,
 63-65
newspapers, **46,** 81
Nipawin, 102
North Battleford, 20, **31,** 89, 112
North-West Mounted Police, 18,
 35, 35, 38-39, 98. *See also* Royal
 Canadian Mounted Police
North-West Territories, 34, 114
North-West Territories Act, 35, 71
Northern Pikes, **88,** 89
Northwest Rebellion, 32, 37-43,
 101, 111, 114
Norwegians, 18
oil, 61, 63, 73, 76, 77-78, 109, 115
Oliver, Frank, 49
Ontario, 36, 47, 77
Organization of Saskatchewan
 Arts Councils, 83
Osika, Ron, 64
Otter, William, 41
Oxbow, 45
Palliser, John, 33
Palliser Triangle, 33, 37
Patterson, W.J., 119-20
park belt, 9, 12, 33
parks, 90, 99-103, 107, 110-12
Parliament, seats in, 46, 67, 108
Pelican Narrows, 103, 112
Perehudoff, William, 87
Peterson, Sandra, 91
petroglyphs, 24, 99, **100,** 111
pictographs, **24,** 24
plants, 27, 107
police, 68
population, 17-21, 105-6
potash, 61, 63, 73, **77,** 77, 109, 115
Potash Corporation of
 Saskatchewan, 63
Poundmaker, 38, 40, **41,** 42, 101,
 120, 120
Powwow, North Battleford, **31**
prairie, 7, **11,** 11-12, 15, 106

prairie dog, **15,** 15, 107
precipitation, 14, 107, **124**
prehistoric times, 9-11, 14
premiers, 59, 62, 63, 64, 121
Prince Albert, 20, 37, 38, **51,** 101, 105
Prince Albert National Park, **13, 90, 102,** 102, 107, 112
pronghorn, **15,** 15
Protestants, 20, 21, 71
provincehood, 48-49, 67, 105
pulp mills, 79, **80**
Qu'Appelle River, 106
Qu'Appelle Valley, 45, 99
radio, 55, 81
railways, 18, 35, 37, 49, 80, 114
Ramsland, Sarah, 53, 120
Reed, George, 90, 120
Regina, **5,** 17, 19, 20, 37, 45, 46-47, 50, **54, 59, 67,** 68, 78, 79, 80, 85, 86, 89, **93,** 94-96, **95,** 105
Regina Cyclone, 91, 110
Regina Folk Festival, 88, 96, 110
Regina Manifesto, 59
Regina Mosaic, 19, **20**
Regina Riot, **56,** 56-57
Regina Symphony, **87,** 87-88
Reindeer Lake, 13, 106
religions, 20-21, 25
reserves, 19, 30, 35, 37
Richardson, **44**
Richardson, Ernie, 91, 120
Riel, Louis, 38-43, **43,** 96, **120,** 120
rivers, 13, 106
Romanians, 45
Romanow, Roy, 64
Ross, Sinclair, 84, **120,** 120
Royal Canadian Mounted Police, 57, 68, **69.** *See also* North-West Mounted Police
Royal Canadian Mounted Police Academy, 68, 69, 96
Royal Canadian Mounted Police Museum, 89, 110, 112-13
Royal Saskatchewan Museum, 10, 89, 96, 113
Rupert's Land, 28, 33
Russians, 18, 47
St. Victor, 99, 111
Sainte-Marie, Buffy, **88,** 89, **120,** 120

Salemka, Irene, 89
Saltcoats, 47
Sapp, Allen, 87, 112, 120
Saskatchewan Arts Board, 83
Saskatchewan Drama League, 85
Saskatchewan Grain Growers Association, 52, 53
Saskatchewan Hospitalization Plan, 60
Saskatchewan Indian Federated College, 31, 64, **70**
Saskatchewan Music Festival Association, 88, 109
Saskatchewan River, 13, 101, 106
Saskatchewan Roughriders, 90-91, **91,** 110
Saskatchewan Science Centre, **95**
Saskatchewan Sports Hall of Fame, 89, 96
Saskatchewan Wheat Pool, 52, 114
Saskatoon, 14, 17, 19, 20, 62, 68, 80, 85, **86,** 86-87, 89, 94, **97,** 97-98, 105
Saskatoon Jazz Festival, 88, 110
Saskatoon Native Theatre, **85**
Saskatoon Riot, 91, 110
Saskatoon Symphony Orchestra, 70, 88
SaskOil, 63
SaskPower, 64, 78
SaskTel, 81
Scandinavians, 18, **19,** 20, 45
Scott, Thomas Walter, 49, 53
Second World War, 57
service sector, 109
settlers, 17-18, **19,** 29, 33-38, 45-49
Shakespeare on the Saskatchewan Festival, **85,** 85
Sifton, Clifford, 47
Siggins, Maggie, 43
Snowbirds, **92**
social reform, 53-54
Spence, Bette, **70**
sports, 90-91, 110
Stanley Mission, **34,** 103, 111
Stoneys, 41
Suffrage, 53
Suknaski, Andy, 120-21
Sures, Jack, 87
Swedes, 18
Swift Current, 37

Symons, R.D., 87
taxes, 69
telephones, 55, 81
television, 81
Temperance, 53, 97
Thatcher, Ross, 62, 63
Thauberger, David, 87
theatre, **85,** 85, 110
time zone, 107
tipi rings, **24,** 24-25
topography, 11-12, 106-7, **122**
tourism, 81, 109
trade, 25, 28-30, 78-79, 109
transportation, **54,** 80
trapping, 79
tree, provincial, **104,** 105
Ukrainians, 18, 19, 20, 45, 47, 98
University of Regina, 64, 96, 115
University of Saskatchewan, 97, 114
uranium, 61, 73, 77, 109, 115
Uranium City, 103
Val Marie, 15
Vanderhaege, Guy, 85, 121
Veregin, 102, 112
Verigin, Peter, **121,** 121
Vickers, Jon, 89, 121
Victoria Park, 43, 57
visual arts, 86-87
Waltons, the, 89
Wanuskewin Heritage Park, 89, **113,** 113
Warren, Dianne, 85
Wascana Centre, **58,** 95-96, **108**
Wascana Lake, **93, 95,** 96
Weldon, 20
Western Development Museums, **21,** 89, 98, **111,** 113
Weyburn, 100
wheat, 7, 51-52, 55-56, 73, 75, 109
Wiebe, Rudy, 83
Willow Bunch, 88
Wollaston Lake, 13, 106
Wood Mountain, 99
Wood Mountain Post, 112
Worobetz, Stephen, **121,** 121
writers, 83, 84-85
Wynyard, 20
Yorkton, 19, 21, 45, 47, 86, 89, 101, 110
Zenon Park, 20

About the Author

Dave Margoshes is a fiction writer, poet and journalist who lives in Regina, where he works as a freelancer and as a teacher of writing and literature. He graduated from the University of Iowa with an M.F.A. and worked on newspapers in the U.S. and Canada for many years, most recently in Calgary and Vancouver. He has written five books of fiction and poetry; the most recent, *Long Distance Calls*, a collection of short stories, was published in 1996. In 1996, he also won the Stephen Leacock Poetry Award for *The Persistent Suitor*, a poem about death's persistent courtship of a female cancer patient.